BABY, THAT WAS ROCK & ROLL
The Legendary Leiber & Stoller

BABY, THAT WAS

The Legendary

ROCK & ROLL
Leiber & Stoller

Introduction by John Lahr

Text by Robert Palmer

 A Harvest/HBJ Book   Harcourt Brace Jovanovich   New York and London

Printed in the United States of America

Library of Congress Cataloging in Publication Data

Palmer, Robert.
  Baby, that was rock 'n roll.

  (A Harvest/HBJ book)
  1. Leiber, Jerry. 2. Stoller, Mike.
3. Rock musicians—United States—Biography.
4. Rock music—United States—Texts. I. Leiber,
Jerry. II. Stoller, Mike. III. Title.
ML390.P157   784'.092'2   78-7102

ISBN 0-15-610155-6

First edition

B C D E

The authors wish to thank the publishers for permission to quote from the following songs:

Jailhouse Rock © 1957 Gladys Music
Girls, Girls, Girls © 1961 Chappell & Co., Inc., Gladys Music, & Quintet Music, Inc.
Bossa Nova, Baby © 1962 & 1963 Gladys Music
Loving You © 1957 Gladys Music
Treat Me Nice © 1957 Gladys Music
Love Me © 1954 Chappell & Co., Inc., Quintet Music, Inc. & Bienstock Publ. Co.
Trouble © 1958 Gladys Music
Just Tell Her Jim Said Hello © 1962 Gladys Music
Dirty, Dirty Feelin' © 1960 Gladys Music
Don't © 1957 & 1958, Gladys Music
Santa Claus Is Back in Town © 1957 Gladys Music
(You're So Square) Baby, I Don't Care © 1957 Gladys Music
I'm A Woman © 1961 Yellow Dog Music, Inc.
Hound Dog © 1953 & 1956 Gladys Music & American Broadcasting Music, Inc.
Kansas City © 1952 & 1959 Halnat Pub. Co.
Searchin' © 1957 Chappell & Co., Inc., Quintet Music, Inc. & Bienstock Publ. Co.
Down in Mexico © 1956 Chappell & Co., Inc., Quintet Music, Inc. & Bienstock Publ. Co.
Little Egypt © 1961 Chappell & Co., Inc., Gladys Music, & Quintet Music, Inc.
Young Blood © 1957 Unichappell Music, Inc., Trio Music Co., Inc. & Freddy Bienstock Music Co.
The Shadow Knows © 1958 Chappell & Co., Inc., Quintet Music, Inc. & Bienstock Publ. Co.
That Is Rock n' Roll, © 1959 Chappell & Co., Inc., Quintet Music, Inc. & Bienstock Publ. Co.
Run Red Run © 1959 Chappell & Co., Inc., Quintet Music, Inc. & Bienstock Publ. Co.
Soul Pad © 1967 Yellow Dog Music, Inc.
Down Home Girl © 1964 Yellow Dog Music, Inc.
Yakety Yak © 1958 Chappell & Co., Inc., Quintet Music, Inc. & Bienstock Publ. Co.
Along Came Jones © 1959 Chappel & Co., Inc., Quintet Music, Inc. & Bienstock Publ. Co.
Poison Ivy © 1959 Chappell & Co., Inc., Quintet Music, Inc. & Bienstock Publ. Co.
The Climb © 1962 Chappell & Co., Inc., Gladys Music, & Quintet Music, Inc.
Charlie Brown © 1959 Chappell & Co., Inc., Quintet Music, Inc. & Bienstock Publ. Co.
D. W. Washburn © 1968 Screen Gems—EMI Music Inc.
What Is the Secret of Your Success © 1957 Chappell & Co., Inc., Quintet Music, Inc., & Bienstock Publ. Co.
Black Denim Trousers and Motorcycle Boots © 1955 Quintet Music, Inc. & Bienstock Publ. Co.
Framed © 1954 Quintet Music, Inc. & Bienstock Publ. Co.
Riot in Cell Block #9 © 1954 Quintet Music, Inc. & Bienstock Publ. Co.
Smokey Joe's Cafe © 1955 Quintet Music, Inc. & Bienstock Publ. Co.
Alligator Wine © 1958 Quintet Music, Inc. & Bienstock Publ. Co.
Love Potion #9 © 1959 & 1977 Quintet Music, Inc. & Bienstock Publ. Co.
Saved © 1961 Chappell & Co., Inc. & Quintet Music, Inc.
Don Juan © 1961 Chappell & Co., Inc. & Quintet Music, Inc.
Spanish Harlem © 1960 & 1961 Trio Music Co., Inc. and Unichappell Music, Inc.
On Broadway © 1962 & 1963 Screen Gems—EMI Music Inc.
Destination Love © 1956 Chappell & Co., Inc., Quintet Music, Inc. & Bienstock Publ. Co.
Lucky Lips © 1957 Chappell & Co., Inc., Quintet Music, Inc. & Bienstock Publ. Co.
Teach Me How to Shimmy © 1961 Chappell & Co., Inc. & Quintet Music, Inc.
Hard Times © 1952 Travis Music Co.
Nosey Joe © 1952 Regent Music Corp.
Snow Is Fallin' © 1978 Yellow Dog Music, Inc.
Three Time Loser © 1953 Quintet Music, Inc. & Bienstock Publ. Co.
Ruby Baby © 1955 & 1963 Chappell & Co., Inc., Quintet Music, Inc. & Bienstock Publ. Co.
I Keep Forgettin' © 1962 & 1975 Yellow Dog Music, Inc.
I (Who Have Nothing) © 1961 & 1963 Radio Record Ricordi
Saved © 1961 Chappell & Co., Inc. & Quintet Music, Inc.
The Chicken and the Hawk © 1955 Chappell & Co., Inc., Quintet Music, Inc. & Bienstock Publ. Co.
Mainliner © 1952 Arnel Music Corp.
Is That All There Is? © 1966, 1969 Yellow Dog Music, Inc.
Real Ugly Woman, Courtesy of Modern Music

Discographies assembled by Robert Bienstock and Faith Whitehill Koeppel

Special thanks to Ralph Newman, publisher of *Time Barrier Express,* and Arthur Berlowitz for their help in obtaining many of the photographs used in the book.

For Lester Sill

BABY, THAT WAS ROCK & ROLL
The Legendary Leiber & Stoller

ENTER LEIBER AND STOLLER

By John Lahr

It's 1957, a Sunday. Over the last five years, it has become the center of the household. All the furniture in the bedroom faces it. Dad watches it from his desk; Mom from the bed; Sis from the floor. I'm usually on the sofa. Sunday is reserved not for Church, but for Television. Ed Sullivan grins stiffly, promises "a really great *shew*" and, courtesy of Lincoln-Mercury dealers, provides our communion with the rest of America. Athletes, singers, politicians, comedians parade across his stage—all part of our diet of distraction, their well-scrubbed, successful smiles reassuring us that we are part of the club.

Tonight is special. There's a notorious singer on TV, and danger is in the air. CBS has already decreed that he may be televised only from the waist up. What is there below the belt of this country boy with the unforgettable name of Elvis Presley that can't be shown to us city folk? I mean, we've seen murder on "Dragnet," we've seen Senator McCarthy on the "Six O'Clock News" waving an envelope with the names of card-carrying Communists, we've seen Uncle Miltie in panties and bra, and we've ogled Marilyn Monroe's cleavage.

In the suspenseful moments before his appearance, Mom studies the Presley LP we made her buy. Dad just shakes his head. He's watched Sis and me dance to Elvis after dinner, and he's listened in disbelief. "What's happened to show business standards?" he says. "Jerry Vale. Now, there's a voice. You kids want to hear a performer? Get out the Billy Daniels records."

Suddenly Elvis is in front of us. He's been cleaned up for the TV audience. He's exchanged black leather for silver lamé. He stands there sparkling, with his guitar slung across his stomach like a machine gun as the squeals from the audience subside. His lips are poised between a seductive pant and an insolent smirk. He nods to the sidemen, steps up to the microphone, and unleashes a sound that pierces our viscera like a shot of Vitamin B.

You ain't nothin' but a hound dog
Cryin' all the time
You ain't nothin' but a hound dog
Cryin' all the time
Well, you never caught a rabbit
And you ain't no friend of mine

A black curl lashes his forehead as he starts his censored wiggle. This is where I lose control—

knocked out of my seat by his kinetic outrageousness. Sprawled on the floor, I can't believe my eyes. Even Dad is having a ball.

On the way to bed, I pick up the Presley LP. There, in small type, in a parenthesis beside "Hound Dog," are the names J. Leiber/M. Stoller. A few years later, Dad would hand me a *Variety* clipping about them: at twenty-six, they were pop music's wunderkinder. They'd been writing for less than a decade and their songs had already been on over 40 million records, which was more than Jerome Kern's lifetime output.

"You kids were right about 'Hound Dog,'" Dad said. It may have taken Dad a few years to come around, but I knew the minute I saw Elvis on Ed Sullivan that rock & roll was here to stay.

Rock & roll was rogue energy—it yanked us on our feet and made us move, stomping the floor to its strong backbeat. Leiber and Stoller's songs were potent because they teased our longing with such sly precision. Heavily sedated with a stiff dose of '50's conformity, we were nice kids studying hard to succeed, and they—*they* were making fables about renegades. Presley was the original bad guy—the kind of "greaser" our parents told us not to talk to and whom we'd cross the street to avoid. His black leather pants were a little snugger than our Brooks Brothers' charcoal grays. It was even rumored that he didn't wear underwear when he sang.

Leiber and Stoller, who weren't all that much older than we, wrote songs that mined our deepest vein of fantasy. Timid though we were, we could sing along, buoyed up by Elvis's sheer bravado.

You lookin' for trouble?
You come to the right place
You lookin' for trouble?
Just look right in my face
I was born standin' up and talkin' back
My daddy was a green-eyed mountain Jack
And I'm evil
Evil as can be
You know I'm evil
So don't you mess around with me

"Trouble" was not exactly the kind of song they played at dancing school.

Leiber and Stoller took us out of our routine world into a world where sound buzzed through our bodies and words flashed strange pictures of people and places we would never have thought worthy of song: a jailhouse—"Jailhouse Rock," a stripper and her show—"Little Egypt," a motorcycle rebel—"Black Denim Trousers and Motorcycle Boots" wherein they perpetrate a myth as offensive to adults as it was exciting to adolescents.

Well, he never washed his face
And he never combed his hair
He had axle grease imbedded underneath his
*   fingernails*
On the muscle of his arm was a red tattoo,
A picture of a heart
Sayin', 'Mother I Love You.'

Did Leiber and Stoller imagine us listening to the radio with lights out, playing pocket pool on our beds, rehearsing how to jimmy a Maiden Form bra with thumb and forefinger? Our hunger was too deep for words. Rock & roll alone spoke kindly to our appetites and answered our craving for sensation. Voices—a kind of voodoo? —whispered to us in the darkness, "Shoodooten Shoo–be–dah." And we answered back.

The movies overloaded our circuits with virginal pony tails: Sandra Dee, Debbie Reynolds, Annette Funicello. Cole Porter had told us breezily that love was "de-lovely" and the Gershwins told us, equally elegantly, that passion was " 'Swonderful." Theirs was clean, unphysical sex. But rock & roll was hot and horny. That saxophone was downright low-down. It made connections with the body. When Elvis crooned Leiber and Stoller's "Don't" and "Love Me," he wasn't issuing an invitation to the waltz. Leiber and Stoller knew that what we wanted was sex. Little Egypt's "Ying-Yang Ying-Yang" spoke to us in the language of our

private dreams of sexual glory. Her kind of woman never got into a Patti Page song!

I went and bought myself a ticket and I sat
*   down in the very first row–oh–oh*
They pulled the curtain up and when they
*   turned the spotlight way down low–oh–oh*
Little Egypt came out struttin', wearin' nuttin'
*   but a button and a bow–oh–oh*
Singin', "Ying–yang, ying–yang . . ."

It was flesh we craved. We would risk anything—even contamination—for a touch and tickle. In "Poison Ivy," Leiber and Stoller isolated that itch and our yearning to scratch it. They created a woman who could make us suffer for our dirty little dreams. (And we loved it.)

She comes on like a rose
But everybody knows
She'll get you in dutch
You can look but you better not touch
Poison Ivy, Poison Ivy
Late at night while you're sleepin'
Poison Ivy comes a-creepin' around

Our sexual anticipation was as outrageous and hilarious as the song's remedy for it.

You're gonna need an ocean
Of calamine lotion

Conquest was our only concern. Even before we'd heard of erogenous zones, we talked endlessly about aphrodisiacs. Mushrooms and asparagus tips were rumored to loosen up the libido, and Spanish Fly to drive girls into an uncontrollable frenzy. We wouldn't have to pitch them. We wouldn't even have to feel guilty afterwards since they wouldn't remember a thing. In fact, we would be doing them a favor by putting them out of their sexual misery—better us than the stick shift of the Chevrolet. We wanted sexual success and no stigma—in other words, magic. "Love Potion #9 gently mocked that daydream. What the singer confessed to the Gypsy with the gold-capped tooth, we would never have admitted to ourselves.

I told her that I was a flop with chicks
I been this way since nineteen fifty-six
She looked at my palm, and she made a
*   magic sign*
She said: What you need is—Love Potion #9

"Love Potion #9" didn't take our embarrassment as seriously as we couldn't help taking it. We could be singing to ourselves and suddenly find tears in our eyes. "Kansas City," for instance, promised us everything we ever wanted—movement, sex, and satisfaction.

I'm goin' to Kansas City
Kansas City here I come

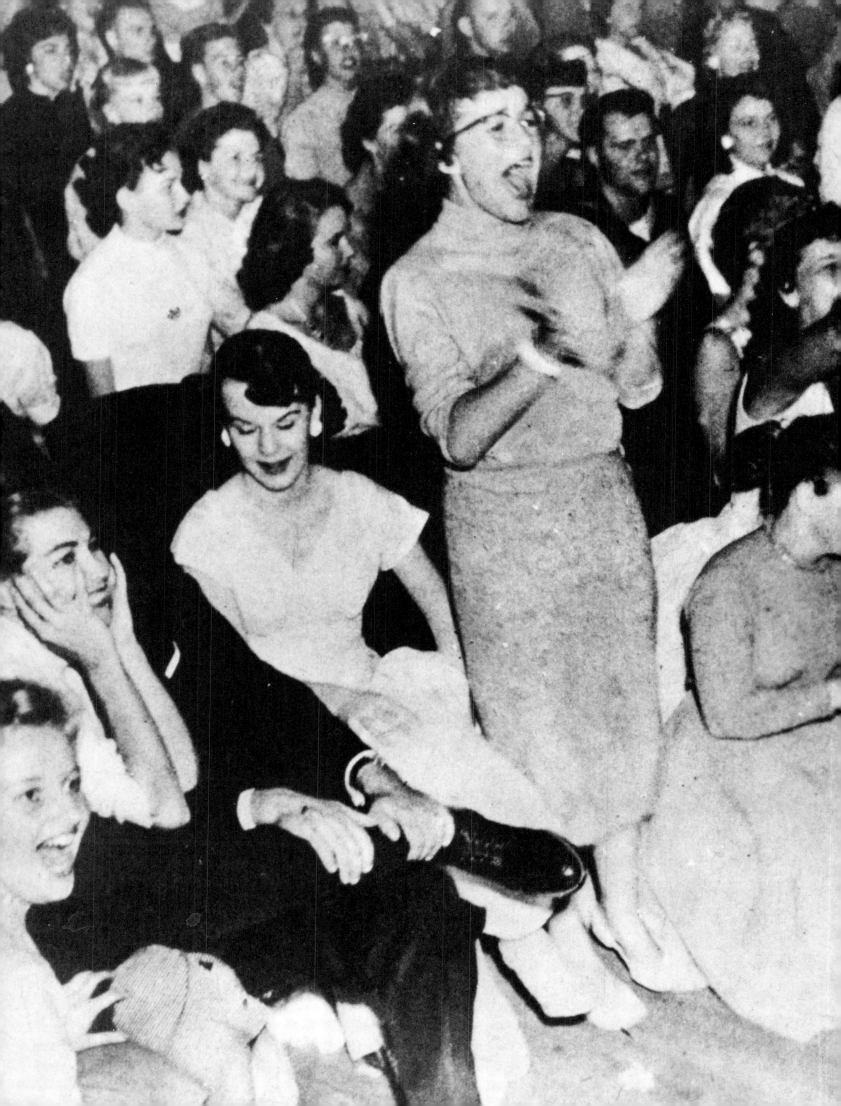

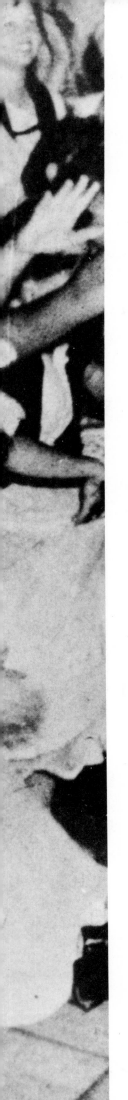

They got a crazy way of lovin' there
And I'm gonna get me some

Whether we were cruising for poon in Dad's car with the radio blaring, dancing silently in front of a mirror, or walking home alone after a date, "Kansas City" was in our ears, filling us with hope. We spent the '50's wishing—for school to end, for women, for life with a capital L to begin. The world was out there. Any day now, we would be able to reach out and actually taste it. Suddenly there would be nothing to stop us.

Well, I might take a train
I might take a plane
But if I have to walk
I'm goin' just the same

Rock & roll was usually long on good times and short on humor. Laughter admitted failure, which killed passion—and what adolescent could stand that? Most of the songs we listened to were in dumb earnest—a few repeated phrases interrupted by a wailing saxophone and an occasional rim shot on the drums. But Leiber and Stoller's songs played with us; many of them were tales in verse, with a surprising antic quality to them. The Coasters made these routines into standards. Leiber has described the Coasters as "a group of vaude-villians, all of them comedians." So were Leiber and Stoller—they could make us laugh at our loneliness ("Searchin' "), at our sexual frustration ("Love Potion #9"), at our rebellious goofing off ("Charlie Brown"), at our bossy parents ("Yakety Yak"). These songs were dramatic events in which a character and a problem were established and then comically elaborated on, as when the boy who had gone looking for the love potion described swallowing it.

It smelled like turpentine
  And looked like India ink.
I held my nose
I closed my eyes
I took a drink.

The scene that began realistically—then exploded with slapstick.

I didn't know if it was day or night
I started kissin' everything in sight
But when I kissed the cop down at Thirty-
  Fourth and Vine
He broke my little bottle of Love Potion #9

With plot and dialogue, "Yakety Yak" lured the listener into the middle of family drama: nagging parents vs. captive children whose protest could be expressed only in code ("yakety yak"). Each role in the song amounted to a neat verbal impersonation.

You just put on your coat and hat
And walk yourself to the laundromat
And when you finish doin' that
Bring in the dog and put out the cat.
Yakety yak!
"Don't talk back."

The characters who strutted through Leiber and Stoller's comic songs were flamboyant poseurs, making spectacles of themselves and straight-arming the adult world.

Who walks in the classroom cool and slow?
Who calls the English teacher Daddy-O?
Charlie Brown
Charlie Brown
He's a clown
That Charlie Brown

We kids were just as theatrical as Charlie Brown, if not as bold. With grown-ups, we could try on mock outrage. Like Charlie, we chanted: "Why is everybody always pickin' on me?" But we always knew what we'd done wrong—making prank phone calls, snowballing busses, dropping water bombs, sneaking copies of *Playboy* off the newsstand when mischief raced our engine. But too often we were timid; and how we hated ourselves for acting the innocent child when the finger was pointed at us.

Who's always writin' on the walls?
Who's always goofin' in the halls?
Who's always throwin' spit balls?
Guess who?
"Who me?"
Yeah, you

We worried about being "cool" and looking lethal. We logged hours in front of the mirror—testing our smiles, our smirks, our hair, our walk. Our world was divided into Tweeds and Greasers, both wanting to be "tough" and irresistible. The Tweeds were would-be Ivy Leaguers who bought Hollywood's Tab Hunter—Robert Wagner hard-sell—white bucks, khaki pants, button-down shirt, red-striped tie. We were shiny, formal, and eager. We trusted our facade to work for us as successfully as it had worked for our film heroes. They wore make-up; we had Clearasil. We wanted to be perfect. The Greasers swallowed James Dean and Marlon Brando whole. They were big on silence and scruffiness. They were losers in life, and, what's more, they didn't care; they gloried in it. That's why they were dangerous—they had nothing to lose. With their leather jackets, DA's, T-shirts with cigarette packs rolled in the turned-up sleeves, they wanted to be left alone. We wanted to be accepted.

The movies suited us perfectly. Nothing else was big enough or pure enough. "Searchin' " went to the core of this mystique. Behind our show of style and whispered words of passion was a movie paradigm.

Well, Sherlock Holmes, Sam Spade, got
nothing, child, on me
Sergeant Friday, Charlie Chan and Boston
Blackie
No matter where she's hidin' she's gonna
hear me comin'
I'm gonna walk right down that street like
Bulldog Drummon'
'Cause I've been searchin'
Searchin'—oh, yeah
Searchin' every which a-way
But I'm like that Northwest Mountie
You know I'll bring her in some day

"Searchin' " made us laugh because it was impudent and surprising. Leiber and Stoller were making music of the Grade-B film detectives our parents pooh-poohed as "wastes of time." Along with Chuck Berry and Little Richard, they made an event out of language as well as music.

Measles make you bumpy
And mumps'll make you lumpy
And chicken pox'll make you jump and twitch
A common cold'll fool ya
And whoopin' cough can cool ya
But Poison Ivy, Lord'll make you itch.

While we fumbled to describe our experiences, Leiber and Stoller were always right on target. They didn't waffle. Look at "Along Came Jones," their parody of cowboy melodrama.

I got so bugged I turned it off an' turned on
another show
But there was the same old shoot-'em-up and
the same old rodeo
Salty Sam was tryin' to stuff Sweet Sue in a
burlap sack
He said, "If you don't gimme the deed to your
ranch I'm gonna throw you on the railroad
track."

And then he grabbed her.
And then?
He tied her up.
And then?
He threw her on the railroad track.
And then?
A train started comin'.
And then, and then, and then? . . .

And then along came Jones
Tall thin Jones
Slow walkin' Jones
Slow talkin' Jones
Along came long, lean, lanky Jones.

Leiber and Stoller spoke to our profoundest yearnings and told our story to the world with a wit that made it listen. They corrupted us with pleasure. "Yakety Yak," "Poison Ivy," "Charlie Brown," "Kansas City," and so many others were more than art—they were life. Dancing and laughing, we came of age to their songs.

LEIBER AND STOLLER:
THE ROCK & ROLL YEARS
By Robert Palmer

Jerry Leiber and Mike Stoller were just twenty-three years old on September 9, 1956, when Elvis Presley capped his already incendiary performance on the Ed Sullivan show by dead-panning an introduction—"Friends, as a great philosopher once said. . ."—and imprinting one glorious, snarling verse of "Hound Dog" on the consciousness of America. But the song had already been a hit among black people, in an even more snarling version by Willie Mae "Big Mama" Thornton, and Jerry and Mike already had five years of professional songwriting, be-hind them—almost exclusively for a black au-dience. They were to leave an even more profound imprint on rock & roll, and on the broader spectrum of American popular music. But on that night in 1956, Elvis Presley and Lei-ber and Stoller's "Hound Dog" were rock & roll. Young Americans everywhere could tell in-stinctively that a cultural flash-point had been reached; they would never be quite the same again.

Leiber and Stoller began by composing—Jerry wrote the words and Mike the music, with occasional overlap—some of the most success-ful rhythm-and-blues songs of the early 1950's. In those days, rhythm and blues was a euphe-mism for black popular music, which ranged from the down-home Mississippi blues of Muddy Waters to the urbane doo-wop vocals of the Ravens and Orioles. Jerry and Mike, working in Los Angeles, tailored their songs to a variety of artists. Big Mama Thornton's "Hound Dog," released in 1953, had a Texas-Louisiana country feel. "K.C. Loving," re-corded by Little Willie Littlefield in 1952 and subsequently made famous as "Kansas City" by Wilbert Harrison, was in a city boogie style. Regional and rural-urban distinctions were still important; radio was largely a local phenom-enon, not yet a primarily network affair, and television was just beginning to catch on. Leiber used his remarkable ear for linguistic nuance to capture the verbal idioms of South-westerners and Southerners, city and country folk, while Stoller crafted catchy melodies and any kind of arrangement necessary to suit a particular singer or band. By 1956, when Pres-ley's recording of "Hound Dog" made their rep-utation outside the insular world of black music, Leiber and Stoller had written for Ray Charles, Jimmy Witherspoon, Little Esther, the Robins, the Drifters, Joe Turner, and Ruth Brown,

among many others. With Presley's help, they injected some of the gritty street philosophy and insistently physical rhythms of black music into the mainstream of American pop.

But Leiber and Stoller were more than song-writers, and it is that "more" which distin-guishes them from the songwriters of previous decades and makes them so very important. As they both are fond of saying, "We didn't write songs, we wrote records." A simple enough statement, perhaps, but its implications pro-foundly altered the development of American music.

Before Leiber and Stoller, before rock & roll, popular records were made by bureaucracies. Somebody wrote a song, somebody else wrote an arrangement, and then an Artists and Rep-ertoire, or A&R, man employed by a record company hired musicians and a studio for the recording session. Most of the men who made rhythm-and-blues or country-and-western rec-ords were the owners of one-man operations. Sometimes they produced records themselves and sometimes they hired producers, but they rarely wrote the material. Leiber and Stoller did everything except sing. They conceived a finished product rather than just words and music. And since they had neither the temper-ament nor the inclination to become cogs in a corporate wheel, or to take the ownership of a small company on their own shoulders, they became the first successful independent record producers in the history of the record busi-ness—men who made records for various com-panies in a free-lance capacity rather than working for one company as A&R men. In forg-ing the first important independent production agreement, they opened the music industry to the talents of the sort of creative people who would never be willing to punch a time clock. At least half of today's popular records are in-dependent productions.

Later, as songwriters and producers for the Coasters vocal group, Leiber and Stoller cre-ated what were arguably the most enduring and hands-down funniest records of the rock 'n roll era—"Along Came Jones," "Yakety Yak," "Charlie Brown," "Searchin'," and the rest. As producers for the Drifters during the early 1960's, they made the first records in a popular genre now referred to as "sweet soul." The Drifters' "Save the Last Dance for Me" and "This Magic Moment," and "Spanish Harlem" and "Stand by Me" by Drifters lead singer Ben E. King, grafted intense black vocals onto a back-ground of African and Latin percussion and swirling violins, creating a trend which domi-nates black pop to this day.

Mike at four or five. "When I was sixteen we moved to Los Angeles. That's me at the piano in our apartment on Columbia Avenue. The picture on the wall is a photo of George Gershwin."

Jerry grimacing for a family pose at about nine years old. "I was twelve or fourteen."

From these triumphs, Leiber and Stoller went on to found Red Bird records, which defined the New York pop sound of the mid-1960's through hit recordings by the Shangri-Las, the Dixie Cups, and other girl groups. The arrival of English rock temporarily eclipsed Jerry and Mike, although the Beatles' "Kansas City" and the Rolling Stones' version of "Poison Ivy" were only a few of the many tributes by British rockers to the Leiber-Stoller genius. During the late sixties and early seventies Leiber and Stoller bounced back with top-ten hits for such diverse artists as Procol Harum, Peggy Lee and Stealers Wheel. More recently they received a gold record for their album with English rocker, Elkie Brooks. They are writing for Broadway and have a song in the hit musical "Dancin'."

This tangled synopsis may seem to describe the careers of half a dozen different people, but the differences are more apparent than real. In essence, Leiber and Stoller are conceptual artists whose medium is popular records. It is their influences—black rhythm and blues, ghetto humor, Broadway, the legitimate theater, classical music, Latin rhythms, jazz—which are diverse. And even this cultural smorgasbord is readily comprehensible once one understands who they are and where they came from.

A 1950's magazine article described Jerry Leiber as "bouncy, wordy and uncertain." In fact, he combines the inquisitive intelligence of a born writer—he is legendary at Elaine's, the New York literary hangout—with the street savvy of a man who has moved among both the very poor and the very wealthy. He was born on April 25, 1933, in Baltimore. His father, who had taught in a Hebrew school in Poland, died when he was five, and his mother took the $100 insurance money and opened a candy store on the edge of the black ghetto. Later she turned the place into a grocery, and it became young Jerry's job to carry up 100-pound sacks of potatoes and canned goods from the cellar and to deliver kerosene and soft coal to the homes of black customers.

"My mother was the only one who extended credit to black people," Leiber remembers. "Most of their homes didn't have electricity; they used kerosene lamps. I was very welcome, and I loved to make that trip to their homes. They always made a big fuss over me. I loved the dark rooms with the coal fires, the smells of cabbage and pork cooking—lots of kids to horse around with. A radio was always playing. Those radios were like magic boxes to me; they played music I never heard anywhere else. Sometimes they played Southern country music but mainly they played rhythm and blues."

Jerry Leiber, Lester Sill, Lou Krefetz (Manager of The Clovers), and Mike Stoller posing as a rhythm-and-blues group in front of their Los Angeles office.

With his mother working from dawn until after dark Jerry grew up in the streets. He hung out with a gang, but his best friend was Dunbar, a black kid a few years older. Dunbar wanted to grow up to be a professional boxer, and Jerry wanted to be a drummer and tap dancer. At nine he began taking piano lessons at his Uncle Dave's house ("Uncle Dave who owned a successful grocery," he is quick to point out, "not Uncle Dave the Numbers' King"), but the piano teacher had bad breath. To compound Jerry's problems, Uncle Dave hated the sound of the boogie woogie licks his nephew kept hammering away at. One day Uncle Dave shouted, "Stop banging on the piano or get out of the house!" Jerry left and that was the end of piano lessons.

But Uncle Dave did not give up. He sent Jerry to a Hebrew youth center and insisted that he join a young Zionist group, the Habonim. Today Leiber remembers "a bunch of ugly girls and fat boys holding hands and dancing the *hora*. This was definitely not for me. I had dreams of hand-tailored suits, monogrammed shirts, silk ties, and sleek black Buicks like the one Uncle Dave the Numbers' King rode around in." Fortunately, Jerry was saved from the Habonim and other civilizing influences in 1945, when his mother took him to California on a Greyhound bus. "I'd never seen a palm tree before," he says, "except in a Dorothy Lamour movie. I thought Los Angeles was paradise."

The Leibers moved into an apartment two blocks from the R.K.O.-Paramount lot, and Jerry began haunting the front gate. Being naturally gregarious, he soon made friends with the guards, and eventually he talked himself into Cecil B. DeMille's office and announced that he wanted to be a movie star. DeMille advised him to go to school to study music and drama. Two years later, Jerry was working at the Circle Theater, painting sets, sweeping the theater, and selling Cokes. The repertory included Odets, Saroyan, and Shaw, and although Jerry wanted mightily to act, he was too young for any of the parts. He got bored and began to think about music again. His older sister was married to the son of songwriter Lew Porter, who also scored westerns, and Jerry decided after watching Porter at work that songwriting and composing might be an exciting life.

When he was sixteen, Leiber began working in a record store on Fairfax Avenue. The customers were buying "Mule Train" by Frankie Laine, but Jerry was listening to rhythm and blues. He began jotting down his own blues lyrics in a series of notebooks, but he could not write music so he began searching for a collaborator. "First," he says "I was trying to work with a drummer, a classmate at Fairfax High, but he wasn't really interested in songwriting. He finally suggested that I call a piano player who was studying composition, Mike Stoller."

That fifties magazine article described Stoller as "bearded and shy." According to Leiber he was "withdrawn, practically comatose" when they met, "although," Jerry adds, "he's become more outgoing, and I've become more withdrawn, over the years." Today, Mike radiates a low-keyed but noticeably impulsive sort of intensity. He often lets Leiber do the talking but, when asked, he remembers names, dates, and places with almost unfailing accuracy and is able to place events in perspective with a few well-chosen words.

Mike was born March 13, 1933, little more than a month before Jerry, in Belle Harbor, Long Island, a middle class community near Rockaway Beach. When he was four, the family moved to Sunnyside, part of Long Island City, just across the bridge from Manhattan. His father, who was an engineer and draftsman, worked as a travelling salesmen during the Depression. His mother had been a model and actress and was in the chorus of George Gershwin's "Funny Face." There was a photograph of Gershwin, inscribed to her, near the piano. Mrs. Stoller took Mike to Broadway shows, and his Aunt Ray, who had studied at the Vienna Conservatory, gave him piano lessons. But after a few months, Mike gave up on the lessons. "I couldn't take the discipline," he says. Like Leiber, he would learn a great deal about music without having to study with anyone for very long.

The summer he was seven, Mike heard black children playing boogie woogie on an old upright piano at an interracial summer camp. He began imitating the patterns, and by the time he was eleven he had learned enough to impress a neighbor, who suggested lessons with the great stride pianist and jazz composer James P. Johnson. Johnson showed him more boogie woogie patterns, which was what he was interested in, but soon Mike drifted away from these lessons too and went back to playing boogie and blues by ear. He continued in this vein until, at the age of fourteen, he became intrigued by modern jazz—the bebop of Charlie Parker, Dizzy Gillespie, and Thelonious Monk. Together with his friend Al Levitt, a jazz drummer, Mike would hang out on 52nd Street in New York City, where night clubs like the Three Deuces and the Famous Door constituted the world epicenter of the modern jazz movement. Mike and Al even joined a social club on 124th Street in Harlem.

In 1949, when Mike was sixteen, the family moved to Los Angeles. His father set up a contracting business and machine shop and wanted Mike to work with him, but after he nearly cut off his finger with a bandsaw the budding pianist decided to stick to music. He wanted to be a jazz musician, but he says, "I never thought I had the chops to be a really good player." Through his interest in bebop he had become involved in modern classical music; Bartok and Stravinsky were important influences on the boppers. So Mike shifted his emphasis and began studying composition with Arthur Lange, a Hollywood arranger and film scorer. He wrote several pieces, including a short orchestral work which was performed by the Santa Monica Symphony. Toward the end of the fifties he studied composition again, this time with serialist composer Stefan Wolpe; one of his pieces, "Quartet," was performed in Max Pollikoff's "Music In Our Time" series in New York in 1962.

But Mike was no ivory tower wunderkind. He played piano with pickup bands for dances, and although he insists that his instrumental skills were negligible, he did manage to keep up with the difficult bebop chord changes which were popular among young musicians at the time. On one occasion, at a Fillipino dance in the Alexandria Hotel, he played alongside jazz trumpeter Chet Baker in a mostly Mexican-American band led by his friend Blas Vasquez.

The Stollers lived in a neighborhood which was heavily Mexican-American. "I learned the Pachuco dances and joined a Pachuco social club," Mike recalls. "We wore heavy-soled cordovan shoes, chino pants, Hawaiian shirts." With the Harlem social club behind him, the sixteen-year-old Mike Stoller, who was already enrolled in Los Angeles City College, had the makings of an unusual classical composer. Then one day he got a call from a high school senior who had been referred to him by a mutual friend. The caller announced that his name was Jerome Leiber and that he wanted to collaborate on some songs. "To me," says Mike, "songs meant a lot of junk you heard on the radio, like 'Hold me in your arms and let me thrill to all your charms.' I was very negative. 'I don't want to write songs,' I told him. But he was very persistent."

Leiber was so persistent, in fact, that soon he was standing at Mike's door. He had one brown eye and one blue eye, and Mike just stood there and stared at him until his mother suggested he invite the visitor in. Jerry had brought a school composition book with lyrics pencilled in it, and Mike began thumbing through it listlessly. Then he noticed that there were quite a few ditto marks.

Mike with a beard (left) and Jerry (right) at Dick Charles's recording studio at 729 Seventh Avenue, making a "demo," circa 1958.

Snow is fallin', fallin' on the cold, cold ground
  "   "   "   "   "   "   "   "   "

Gloom and misery, gloom and misery all
  around

The ditto marks were blues repeat lines. "These are blues," Mike said. "I like blues." His favorite blues were mostly the reverse sides of instrumental records by jazz-oriented performers like Eddie "Cleanhead" Vinson and Jay McShann, while Leiber liked the rawer Southern and Southwestern blues, but the form was the same. It was a common ground. Mike took the notebook over to the piano. "I didn't know you were talking about the blues," he said, almost accusingly. He began flipping through the book, playing chords here, boogie woogie figures there. "Yeah," he said finally, "okay, let's write some songs."

It was the summer of 1950. The pair began working at Mike's family's place, a small apartment near downtown L.A. The upright piano was in a corner, with the autographed picture of George Gershwin over it. Mike's fold-down bed was nearby, and the telephone was in a closet. During the first sessions, Mike actually fell asleep on the couch a few times while the hyperactive Jerry was nervously pacing and tossing out an endless stream of lyrics. The problem, Leiber found, was that Mike was taking phenobarbitol for an ulcer he had devel-

oped earlier that year. Despite the medication, says Stoller, "there was some kind of balance in our metabolisms. Jerry's energy motivated me. I could be sprawling on the couch and he would suddenly shout out some words to me, and I would respond."

Leiber describes a typical session. "Often, I would have a start, two lines or four lines. Mike would sit at the piano and start to jam, just playing, fooling around, and I'd throw out a line. He'd accommodate the line—metrically, rhythmically. I would sing some note within the chord he was playing. And we'd move on from there. Often we would just sit down with nothing to go on. He'd start playing and I'd start shouting." Leiber soon discovered that Stoller had a steel trap of a musical memory that was chock full of boogie woogie, blues, and jazz licks, in addition to ideas from the worlds of bebop and classical music. Stoller discovered that Leiber was not just a gifted wordslinger but a natural singer—also, Mike says, a natural dancer—with an unselfconscious delight in the rhythm of word combinations and lines. In fact, Leiber could have been the first successful white blues singer, but the idea never even occurred to Jerry or Mike. "We wanted, above all, to be authentic," says Stoller, "and a white person singing the blues seemed terribly inauthentic to us."

Red Bird

BLUE CAT

Ellie Greenwich and Jeff Barry were song-writers and producers associated with Leiber and Stoller's Red Bird label.

John Hammond, blues singer.

George Goldner, vet-eran record man, was Red Bird's Sales and Promotion Manager.

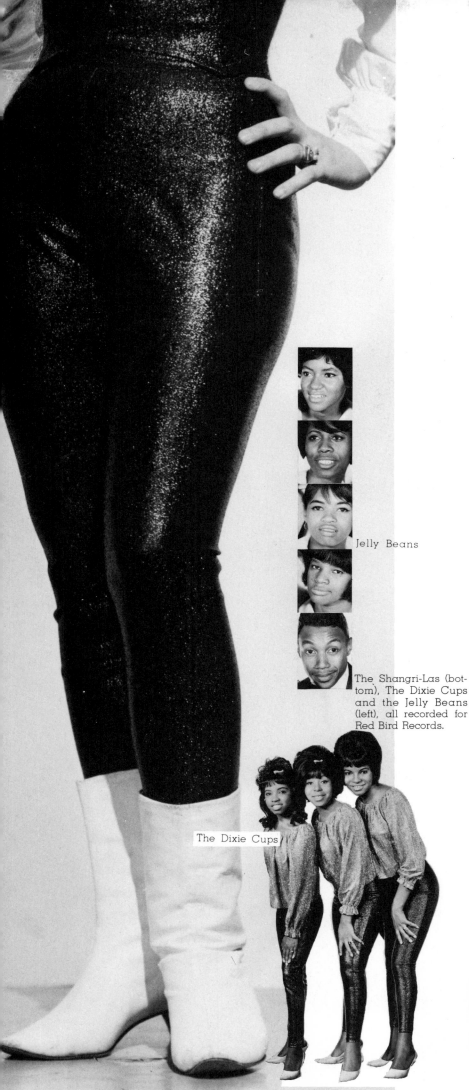

Jelly Beans

The Shangri-Las (bottom), The Dixie Cups and the Jelly Beans (left), all recorded for Red Bird Records.

The Dixie Cups

Through the summer and into the next fall, the two worked on their blues songs and hung out together—double dating, getting drunk, riding around in Stoller's '37 Plymouth. There were dances in the black ghetto, with music by bluesy swing bands like Johnny Otis's and Joe Liggins's, and jazz clubs where some of the great bebop saxophonists—Dexter Gordon, Wardell Gray—worked their magic in all-night jam sessions. More and more, Leiber and Stoller dropped out of conventional white society and began to identify themselves with the black subculture. They moved through a night world populated by jazzmen, black hipsters, and other stylish, creative, economically marginal types.

"We found ourselves writing for black artists," Leiber says, "because those were the voices and rhythms we loved. By the fall of 1950, when both Mike and I were in City College, we had black girlfriends and were into a black lifestyle."

When they began writing together, Leiber and Stoller were concerned above all with sounding authentic, which to them meant exclusively black. But while Jerry continued to conceive his lyrics with traditional blues inflections in mind, Mike felt the need for a bit more musical originality.

The dilemma was solved, and the Leiber-Stoller style of blues writing born, in 1952. Jerry had come up with the words to "K.C. Loving," which was later retitled "Kansas City" and recorded by a staggering number of rock and rhythm-and-blues artists, and he suggested that the music sound traditional, like any number of twelve-bar blues performed by artists such as Memphis Slim and Joe Turner. Stoller disagreed, and to prove his point he came up with the song's catchy melody, which is probably the secret of its lasting appeal. "It's a melodic blues," he says. "If you hear it instrumentally, you'll still recognize that it's 'Kansas City,' not just a blues in F or a blues in C."

But Jerry and Mike were able to have their cake and eat it too, for while the song's jaunty tune put it over with pop listeners, it still sounded enough like a traditional blues to appeal to the blues audience as well. In fact, it was widely assumed to be a folk song in the public domain, and even today it is performed by artists such as Muddy Waters and Albert King right along with traditional blues material.

But we are getting ahead of our story. By the time Leiber and Stoller wrote "Kansas City,"

The Shangri-Las

they had already had a number of songs recorded, and this came about largely through Lester Sill. Jerry met him first, in the record store on Fairfax Avenue. He was the national sales manager for Modern records, an important independent rhythm-and-blues label, and he was wearing one of the sharpest suits Jerry had ever seen. The irrepressible Leiber sang him a few Leiber-Stoller blues, and Sill was impressed. He offered to take the pair around to some of the independent labels which then dominated rhythm and blues, country music, and the other specialized fields which the major labels—Columbia, RCA Victor, and so on—generally left alone. It took several months for them to work up enough confidence in their material, but in 1951 they went to Modern records to audition for the vocal group the Robins.

"The group was there, sitting around the room," Jerry remembers, "and they said, 'Come on, play us some stuff.' Mike played the piano and I sang our song, 'That's What the Good Book Says.' And they said, 'Groovy, yeah, we'll do that.' It was as easy as that. We couldn't believe it. Because the other way to get your songs recorded was Vine Street, the conventional channels of publishing, and you couldn't even get in to see a publisher unless you had some sort of reputation."

Seeing their names on a record—even though they were misspelled *Lieber and Stroller*—gave the pair a sense of real accomplishment and very soon Leiber and Stoller had their names spelled correctly, on a number of rhythm-and-blues hits. But already Jerry and Mike were doing more that just writing songs. "We found," says Mike, "that if we wrote a piece that was to be played as a Texas shuffle, for example, it would more than likely end up sounding like some Mickey Mouse swing record if we weren't there to supervise. And so we became record producers in self defense." "As word got around," Jerry explains, "we got a reputation for not only being songwriters but coming up with little arranging ideas for records. People started to depend on us for these contributions." This degree of involvement was only a step away from record production, and on August 13, 1952, Leiber and Stoller became *de facto* producers when they supervised, from the studio control booth, Big Mama Thornton's recording of their song "Hound Dog."

Johnny Otis, a white drummer and vibraphonist, was the leader of a popular black blues band. He asked Leiber and Stoller to write some material for several of the singers in his band, Little Esther and Big Mama among them. "We went down to a rehearsal," says

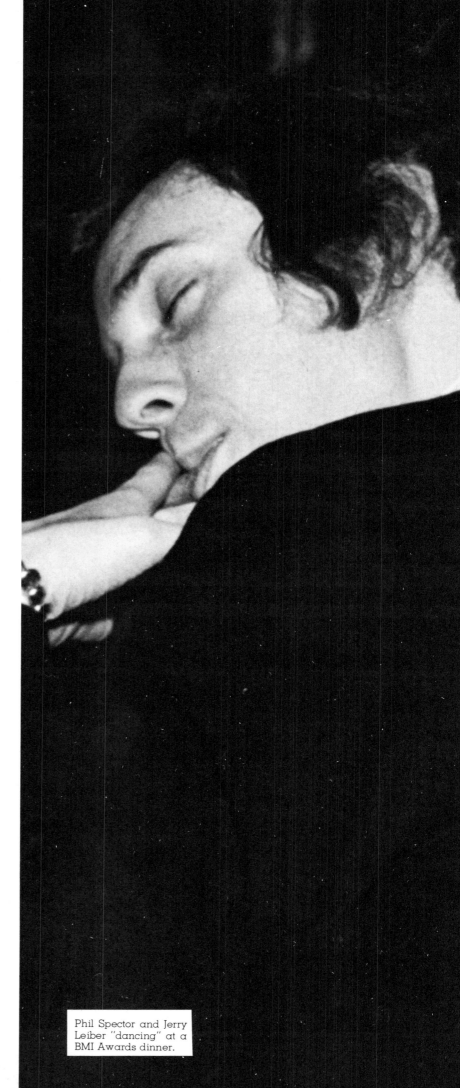

Phil Spector and Jerry Leiber "dancing" at a BMI Awards dinner.

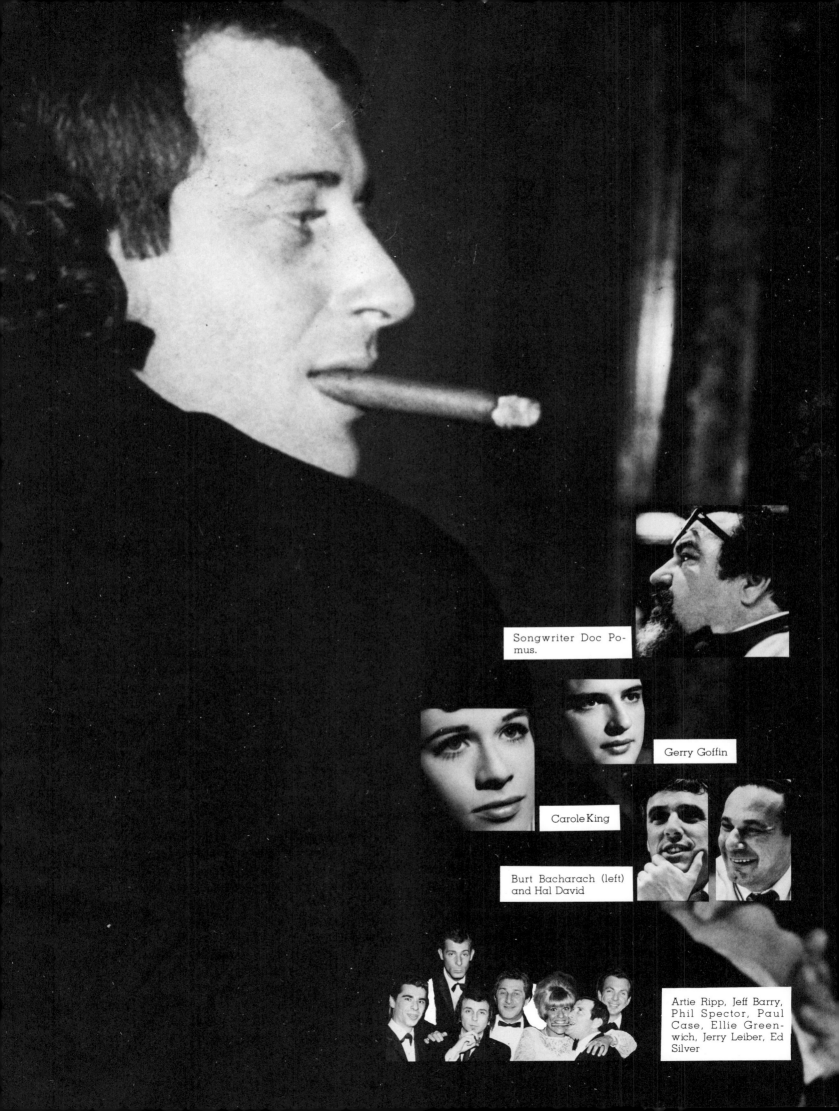

Songwriter Doc Pomus.

Gerry Goffin

Carole King

Burt Bacharach (left) and Hal David

Artie Ripp, Jeff Barry, Phil Spector, Paul Case, Ellie Greenwich, Jerry Leiber, Ed Silver

Above, Stoller (left) and Leiber (right) in a yak pen at the Bronx Zoo, ankle deep in "Yakety Yak."

Leiber, "and watched Big Mama perform. She must have weighed three hundred pounds and she was the saltiest chick we'd ever seen. We went home to write for her and out came 'Hound Dog'."

Otis supervised the recording session first with Leard Bell, who worked with him on the road, playing the drums. The tune had been conceived by Jerry and Mike as a kind of country blues, with the drums playing a loping figure such as one might hear in Louisiana music. Bell had trouble finding a groove, and Jerry and Mike told Otis he had to play drums to save the song. "Who's gonna sit in the booth?" Otis asked. "We will," answered Jerry and Mike. And with Otis on the drums, his snares turned off so that the drum kit got an unusual hollow ring, "Hound Dog" was recorded in two takes. "That was the first time," Leiber says, "that we actually took over some authority and asked for a little bit more of this, a little bit less of that." The record was number one on the national rhythm-and-blues charts for three months, eclipsing the success of Leiber and Stoller's first r&b hit, "Hard Times" by Charles Brown. But since the charts were still segregated, few of Jerry and Mike's remaining white friends heard either tune.

Late in 1953, Jerry, Mike, and Lester Sill started Spark records. Now Leiber and Stoller could produce records officially, and with the help of the same Robins who had recorded "That's What the Good Book Says," they began creating the style of their mature years. The third Spark release, after singles by ex-gospel singers Willy and Ruth and saxophonist Gil Bernal, was an instant classic—the Robins' "Riot in Cell Block #9." The record's rhythmic underpinning was a Delta blues riff lifted from Muddy Waters, but everything else about it was several years ahead of its time. Richard Berry, composer of the immortal "Louie Louie," put in a guest appearance as a tough black convict, narrating the tale of a prison riot with obvious relish. The humor was irreverent and street wise, in the manner of the later Coasters records. "Pass the dynamite," Berry advised, "because the fuse is lit." There were sound effects—sirens, a tommy gun—that might have put the record in a novelty category, but the funky harmony singing and hard blues saxophone by Gil Bernal were serious business. In fact, "Riot" created its own category, the Leiber-Stoller playlet (the term is theirs), a kind of three-minute audio drama with music that would still be the freshest sound on the airwaves years later.

The subsequent Robins hits on Spark—the grimly realistic "Framed," and "Smokey Joe's Cafe," another slice of ghetto reality—were equally creative, but the company had chronic distribution problems. They could sell up to 100,000 copies of a single record in California without breaking out in the rest of the country. Late in 1955, Atlantic records, which had begun as a small independent rhythm-and-blues and jazz label and was prospering with artists like Ray Charles, the Clovers, and Joe Turner, became interested in Spark and its young masterminds. "They were making great r&b records," Atlantic's Jerry Wexler recalls, "very idiomatic records. Not only did the records have intelligent production, they were in tune, had a good beat, and were properly balanced. And the songs also had great penetration, social understanding. Their music had real roots." In Leiber and Stoller, Wexler and Atlantic's President Ahmet Ertegun recognized kindred spirits. They were all young white music lovers who preferred black music to white and were interested in black lifestyles. They were forerunners of the Beat generation, which Jerry and Mike were to find as inauthentic as white blues singers, and prime instigators of the white infatuation with black popular music which was about to ignite the rock & roll era.

When Atlantic made their offer, Jerry and Mike decided that they hadn't really wanted to run a record company anyway. There were too many administrative headaches; they preferred to devote their energies to songwriting and producing. So in 1956 they dissolved Spark and signed their first independent production agreement, with the original Robins' records becoming the property of Atlantic and all future Robins' releases to appear on the company's Atco subsidiary. But there was a fly in the ointment. Some of the Robins didn't like the arrangement, and the group split. Lead singer Carl Gardner and bass singer Bobby Nunn remained with Jerry and Mike, and with the addition of Billy Guy, a brilliant comedy singer, and tenor Leon Hughes, the Coasters, named for the West Coast, were born. Leiber and Stoller worked with the group for several months and in February, 1957, came the double-sided hit single which made the Coasters pop stars, "Searchin' " and "Young Blood."

In his rock & roll history *The Sound of the City* Charlie Gillett calls "Searchin' " "one of the greatest of all rock 'n' roll hits" and "one of the first songs to introduce specific figures from American popular culture." Billy Guy did an inspirational job with Leiber's lyrics, which had him invoking Sgt. Friday, Charlie Chan, Boston Blackie, and the Northwest Mounties, among others, in his search for a missing lady friend. In "Young Blood," Jerry and Mike introduced a device which was to be central to many subsequent Coasters records. There were breaks in which the instruments dropped out and the singers repeated a line one by one in rapid succession. "Looka there," each Coaster marvelled as the "Young Blood" or underage girl walked by, with bass Bobby Nunn finishing off the sequence in a lascivious bumpkin's voice. The effect proved irresistible.

"Searchin' " and "Young Blood" were the last Coasters records made in Los Angeles. In the fall of 1957, Jerry and Mike moved to New York, where they were hired to take charge of RCA Victor's East Coast A&R, with time off for their producing commitments to Atlantic. The RCA job lasted six months. "We never could find our office because they all looked the same," Leiber recalls. "We never made out work sheets; we didn't use requisitions. We really didn't know what they were talking about most of the time." After the RCA debacle the pair freelanced, producing mainly for Atlantic. The Drifters, an Atlantic group which was produced by Ahmet Ertegun and Jerry Wexler, had already turned Leiber-Stoller's "Ruby Baby" and "Fools Fall in Love" into r&b masterpieces.

Elvis Presley, who had signed an exclusive contract with RCA Victor late in 1955 and was turning the country upside down with his versions of rhythm-and-blues oldies and juked-up country tunes, heard their "Hound Dog" in a Las Vegas lounge in 1956 and decided to record it. Being unfamiliar with Big Mama Thornton's original recording, he used the lounge combo's garbled version of the lyrics. "You ain't never caught a rabbit" was not in Leiber and Stoller's original arsenal of invective, but they were not heard to complain.

During the spring of 1956, Stoller and his wife took a European vacation. They booked passage back to New York on the Andrea Doria and, the night before they were to land, the ship was rammed by the Stockholm in a thick fog bank. Mike was carrying a drink into the ballroom when it happened. The Stockholm hit us and went two-thirds of the way through the Andrea Doria, bounced off, and came back in again. The ballroom was enclosed in glass and, after the initial shock, I looked out. It looked like someone had taken a giant letter opener and opened up the side of the boat. The Andrea Doria started listing further and further over on its side, and finally we made it down a jacob's ladder into a lifeboat, which somebody had hacked loose because the winches were broken. Eventually we got onto the Cape

Ann and it took us into New York."

When Leiber heard that the Andrea Doria had been rammed, he spent a frantic night and day trying to find out if Mike had survived. When he learned that the Stollers were among the lucky ones he raced down to the docks to meet them, bringing a silk suit for Mike in case he had been caught without his threads and bubbling with the news that Presley had recorded their song. The news didn't mean much more than the silk suit at first—"I was just happy to see anybody," Mike says—but soon the record was a number-one hit.

Elvis Presley was the right performer at the right moment. He moved and sang much like a black rhythm-and-blues singer. In fact, he was the first white performer to move in a suggestive manner and sing the sort of material that had previously been considered taboo outside the ghetto. He may not have sung the words to Leiber and Stoller's "Hound Dog," but the message of rebellion came through loud and clear, and young people, tired of the platitudes and soft-core euphemisms of the crooners, took the message to heart.

Through Jean and Julian Aberbach, two Viennese entrepreneurs who had founded Hill and Range Music and turned it into one of the most important of the newer music publishing firms, and Freddy Bienstock, who ran the Professional Department at Hill and Range, screened songs for Presley, and later became Leiber and Stoller's business partner, Presley and his manager, Colonel Tom Parker, asked Jerry and Mike to submit more material. Almost immediately Elvis recorded their "Love Me." As sung by Presley, with vocal backing from the Jordanaires, the tune sounds like a white Southern spiritual. It was originally written for the black ex-gospel singers Willy and Ruth, who had recorded in on Spark.

Presley began shooting his first movie, "Love Me Tender," in April, 1957. It was a box-office smash, and as pictures followed in dizzying succession, Jerry and Mike were kept busy supplying material. Among the many tunes they wrote for Elvis's movies were the title songs for such films as *Loving You*, *King Creole*, and *Jailhouse Rock*, in which Mike played the piano player. The work was prestigious; it was the top of the line for pop songwriters during that period. But it was also constricting. "We would get a script marked off where they wanted some type of song," Leiber explains, "like Scene II, Elvis is with so-and-so and needs a love song. The love songs were a great problem, because I really can't write love songs. But that was the least of it. I certainly would never have written a song like 'Jailhouse Rock,' for example, if somebody hadn't said, 'Look,

there's going to be a big production number in a jail.' I think if we hadn't been writing for his films, a lot of the material would have been funkier, freer . . . better."

Encounters with Presley were usually on the run, although Jerry and Mike were still in the habit of being in the studio when their songs were recorded. "He always travelled with an entourage," Jerry says, "and so, in a way, you could say that he never left home. He carried his environment right along with him, so that he was always really insulated from the strange world of Hollywood or wherever. He would have all his buddies in the studio and would stop to crack jokes with them. And he was very high-strung. He would jump to the piano and play a few bars, pick up a guitar, slap somebody on the back, hit three notes on the bass. Then he'd say, 'Okay, let's make it,' and get in front of that microphone and get it in a few takes. His musical instincts and intuitions were just about infallible, and he was one of the most phenomenally consistent performers I've ever seen at work. Rarely did a performance drop in energy. He might prefer one take because of a certain note he hit or a turn of phrase, but they were all good."

Stoller played piano on "Jailhouse Rock," "Treat Me Nice," and a few other songs which went into Presley movies. The Memphis rhythm section of Scotty Moore, Bill Black, and D.J. Fontana was more country oriented than other musicians he had worked with, but they found a common ground in shuffle rhythms. "They were heavy into shuffle," Mike recalls, "and for piano players shuffle is the lazy way to play boogie, 'cause you use both hands instead of getting all the rhythm out of your left hand. So it was easy for me. Of course I didn't know all the white gospel songs that Elvis knew; he knew an awful lot. He knew a lot about what was going on with black musicians too, which was surprising to me, to find another white kid, one even younger than we were, who was aware of people like Ray Charles.

"We were very impressed with him. We were impressed with how good he was. He would do a great take and then insist on another and another and still another. When he was in the mood he could do fifty takes of a number and go on to the next tune without taking a break. To unwind, he'd sit down at the piano and sing a hymn. He never looked at the clock. He would take off half an hour to tell a joke, or send out for sandwiches and orange pop. To us, at the time, that was the height of luxury. We were accustomed to working under pressure in the studio, attempting to make four sides in the allotted three-hour session, in order to avoid paying overtime charges."

"No question about it," says Leiber, "Elvis was the beginning of the revolution in pop music. He had it, whatever you want to call it. TV exposed him to a mass market overnight, but he would have made it, TV or not. He would have made it in the twenties or the thirties or whenever he came on the scene. He was more than a great singer. He was the 'American dream.' "

Elvis was not the only thing on Leiber and Stoller's agenda during the late 1950's—far from it. This was the period of their most intense creativity, when their productions for the Coasters and (beginning in 1959) the Drifters were setting new standards in popular music. There were many other assignments as well. In 1957 alone, Jerry and Mike wrote for Ruth Brown, Eddie Fisher, Perry Como, Julius La Rosa, Clyde McPhatter, Jaye P. Morgan, Screamin' Jay Hawkins, La Vern Baker, Roy Hamilton, and Jack Jones, in addition to the Coasters. Their creativity was lavished primarily on rock & roll, but as professional songwriters they could and did write in almost any style.

There were precedents for the pop playlets Leiber and Stoller developed with the Coasters—radio drama, Leiber's experience in the theater, and a few r&b novelty songs which featured dialogue. But, says Leiber, the main influence was "just attitudes, the way you see something on the street." As discrete works of art—as records—the playlets were as original as anything that flowered in the fifties.

In a sense, the playlets were direct extensions of black ghetto humor. The cool but pointed satire on Hollywood stereotypes in "Along Came Jones," the whiplash verbal exchanges of "Yakety Yak," the down-home exoticism of "Idol With the Golden Head," and the role reversal of "Run, Red, Run," in which a sailor's trained monkey catches him cheating at cards and promises "Red, you made a man out of me, now I'm gonna make a monkey out of you," would not be out of place in a folklorist's collection of black jokes and toasts. But there is a definite progression in the Coasters records, from in-group humor to a more universal and teen oriented sense of fun. The narrator in the Robins' version of "Riot in Cell Block #9," the first record in the playlet style, is like the black folk hero Stagger Lee. He has a sense of humor, but essentially he is tough and remorseless. As the record ends, the riot has been quelled, but our anti-hero indicates that there will be more riots, in a line some rock critics have taken to be a prophecy of the urban violence of the 1960's. The anti-hero in "Charlie Brown," recorded four years after "Riot," is a

fun-loving high school goof-off whose friends admire him even while they anticipate his downfall. "Yakety Yak," another Coasters hit from the late fifties, depicts a conflict between the young and their parents, rather than "Riot's" unstated but implicit conflict between black and white.

"Starting with 'Searchin' ' and its 'pop' imagery," Leiber says, "we started drifting away from exclusively black-oriented rhythm-and-blues subject matter, and after we moved to New York the focus of our work began to shift toward a more universal rock & roll style. It wasn't that we were looking for a larger audience. We were simply doing what we had always done: writing songs that appealed to us. It just so happened that the new material also appealed to a mass audience."

The Coasters' records were the product of intense work. The group—Cornell Gunter had replaced Leon Hughes, and there was a new bass singer, Dub Jones, in place of Bobby Nunn—rehearsed relentlessly with their producers, trying different kinds of timing and getting each lick firmly in place. Billy Guy, the main comedy singer, had a unique imagination, but he also studied the way Leiber sang the songs, often copying it almost note for note. Jerry Wexler maintains that "if you had heard the way Jerry Leiber performed those songs, you would realize that Billy Guy was a surrogate for Jerry's interpretations." Leiber himself tempers this opinion. "Billy Guy was genuinely funny. He had great timing and understood the kind of jokes and points we were trying to make," he says. "The group became comedians as our situation comedies evolved; we sort of grew together."

(As an interesting sidelight, compare Guy's performance on "Searchin' " or "Along Came Jones" to the early Mick Jagger. The resemblances—the constricted throat, the astringent timbre, the slight lisp—are remarkable.)

Stoller wrote the musical arrangements for the Coasters' records and played piano on them. Saxophonist King Curtis, who was as important and personal a voice as the singers, improvised his solos, but his riffing punctuations and comments on the action were written out in advance by Mike. Sometimes an electric guitar was played without an amplifier or George Barnes's banjo was added to the rhythm section for the sort of clattering effect one hears on "Yakety Yak." Mike also arranged the vocal harmonies, which sounded vaguely familiar in the street corner vocal group tradition but often did not conform to conventional gospel or ballad voicings.

On April 24, 1959, Atlantic released "There Goes My Baby," the first Drifters record pro-

1972, Apple Studios in London. Mike and Jerry were producing the British group, Stealers Wheel.

duced by Leiber and Stoller and the first big rock & roll hit which prominently featured strings. Stoller sketched the string arrangement and gave it to Stan Applebaum, who fleshed out the orchestration according to Mike's dictates. But the strings were not the only thing revolutionary about the record. Leiber and Stoller were beginning to experiment with some of the recording techniques which pop producer Phil Spector and a host of other producers and arrangers would later parlay into one of the dominant musical styles of the 1960's and 1970's. In addition to the strings, Drifters records like "Dance with Me," "This Magic Moment," "Save the Last Dance for Me," and "I Count the Tears," all hits in 1959-1960, featured large percussion sections and as many as five guitarists. These elements have become basic ingredients of today's disco records.

"We had one guitar playing 'chicks', eighth-note accents—two or three in each measure," Stoller remembers, "while another guy played a chord and let it ring. There would be a twelve-string and a regular six-string acoustic chugging through, and maybe another guitar playing a figure. The percussion section included African hairy drums, big bowl-shaped affairs with skin heads which still had some of the original animal hair on them, plus a triangel, congas, and a standing tom-tom. Sometimes we used marimbas and other percussion instruments. All this was in addition to the standard drum kit." The rhythm of the records was different, too. It was based on the Brazilian *baion*, which had been popularized by the soundtrack recording from an Italian film, "Anna."

"This Magic Moment" stands as a watershed production. At a certain point in the chorus the orchestra and backup singers drop out completely, leaving the sound of strumming guitars and Ben E. King's achingly soulful voice singing "sweeter than wine/softer than a summer night." Once the voices and strings start up again, they blend into a dense wall of sound. Phil Spector, who was apprenticed to Leiber and Stoller during the early 1960's—he is the guitar soloist on The Drifters' "On Broadway," recorded in 1963—later applied massed orchestral forces and sudden dynamic contrasts to his influential productions on hits by the Crystals, the Ronettes, the Righteous Brothers, and Ike and Tina Turner. But there were differences, and Stoller is quick to give Spector credit for originality. "We had only one drummer and everybody else was on percussion," he says. "Phil was the first to use multiple drum kits, three pianos and so on. We went for much more clarity in terms of instrumental colors, and he deliberately blended everything into a

kind of mulch. He definitely had a different point of view."

Leiber and Stoller wrote only a few of the songs the Drifters sang. They concentrated on their ground-breaking productions (and on their other writing commitments), leaving Drifters songwriting to Doc Pomus–Mort Shuman, Gerry Goffin–Carole King, Barry Mann–Cynthia Weil, and Burt Bacharach–Hal David, four teams that worked in or near the Brill Building, 1619 Broadway in New York, a music business mecca and former headquarters of Tin Pan Alley, where Jerry and Mike still maintain offices. In 1964, when Leiber and Stoller decided to try their hands at running another record label, they cultivated the songwriting talents of Jeff Barry, Ellie Greenwich, and Shadow Morton. It was Morton who came up with the biggest hits on Leiber and Stoller's Red Bird label, producing the Shangri Las' "Leader of the Pack," "Remember (Walking in the Sand)," and "Give Him a Great Big Kiss." Barry, Greenwich, and Phil Spector wrote the Dixie Cups' hit "Chapel of Love," another classic produced by Jerry and Mike. Not everything on Red Bird and its sister label Blue Cat was slinky-girl-group pop. Alvin "Shine" Robinson, a blues guitarist and singer from New Orleans, made two rhythm-and-blues classics for the company, "Somethin' You Got"" and "Down Home Girl." The latter, with a hilarious lyric by Leiber, was later recorded by The Rolling Stones.

From the late fifties through the mid-sixties, Leiber and Stoller encouraged and worked with the brightest writing and producing talents on the scene. For fifteen years, they had written, produced, and supervised the making of hit after hit. In many ways, they were just beginning; they were only thirty-three years old. But their view of the world had begun to change. And in 1966, the year they sold their interest in Red Bird Records, they wrote "Is That All There Is?," a song that clearly pointed to the direction their new work would take. Their "classic period" was over; the Golden Age of Rock & Roll had come to an end.

THE CASH BOX

VOLUME XIV   MAY 30, 1953   NUMBER 36

Best Rhythm 'N Blues Record

HOUSTON—Title of "Best Rhythm 'N Blues Record of 1953" was voted by the nation's operators to the novelty jump, "Hound Dog" by Willie Mae Thornton. Awards went to Don Robey, publisher, prexy of Lion Music and Peacock Records, seen above left, and to Willie Mae, above right.

"It's What's in THE C

THE CASH BOX
Rhythm 'N Blues SLEEPER OF THE WEEK

"HOUND DOG" (2:46) [Lion Pub.]
"NIGHT MARE" (2:47) [Lion Pub.]

WILLIE MAE THORNTON
(Peacock 1612)

WILLIE MAE THORNTON

● Willie Mae Thornton gives a frenzied performance on the top deck, titled, "Hound Dog," and the result is a waxing that will excite and catch itself loads of plays. The tune is a rhythmic Latin tempo middle beat and the thrush belts it dramatically and expressively. Easy when she should be easy, and driving when she has to bang it home. The rhythmic handclapper has just enough of the spiritual feel to stir up the emotions and raise the blood pressure. Flip is a blue mood piece that Willie Mae Thornton sings effectively. The slow beat is an eerie piece with a sad sound. Singer can't throw off the effects of the "nightmare."

Hound Dog

You ain't nothin' but a hound dog, quit snoopin' 'round my door
You ain't nothin' but a hound dog, quit snoopin' 'round my door
You can wag your tail but I ain't gonna feed you no more

You told me you was high class, but I can see through that
You told me you was high class, but I can see through that
And daddy I know, you ain't no real cool cat

You ain't nothin' but a hound dog, quit snoopin' 'round my door
You ain't nothin' but a hound dog, quit snoopin' 'round my door
You can wag your tail but I ain't gonna feed you no more

You made me feel so blue, you make me weep and moan
You made me feel so blue, you made me weep and moan
'Cause you ain't lookin' for a woman, all you lookin' is for a home

You ain't nothin' but a hound dog, quit snoopin' 'round my door
You ain't nothin' but a hound dog, quit snoopin' 'round my door
You can wag your tail but I ain't gonna feed you no more

ONCE IN A LIFE TIME

a record hits the = 1 spot in 11 out of 12 cities on The Cash Box Hot Charts.

The Cash Box, April 18, 1953

in SAN FRANCISCO	in NEWARK	in MEMPHIS
HOUND DOG *Willie Mae Thornton* (Peacock 1612)	**HOUND DOG** *Willie Mae Thornton* (Peacock 1612)	**HOUND DOG** *Willie Mae Thornton* (Peacock 1612)
in DALLAS	in NASHVILLE	in CINCINNATI
HOUND DOG *Willie Mae Thornton* (Peacock 1612)	**HOUND DOG** *Willie Mae Thornton* (Peacock 1612)	**HOUND DOG** *Willie Mae Thornton* (Peacock 1612)
in HARLEM	on CHICAGO'S South Side	in NEW ORLEANS

Willie Mae "Big Mama" Thornton

BEAR CAT

You ain't nuthin' but a bear cat
Scratchin' round my door
You ain't nuthin' but a bear cat
Scratchin' round my door
You can purr, pretty kitty,
But I ain't gonna rub you no more

You said you was a longhair
But I can see thru that
You said you was a longhair
But I can see thru that
And baby I know
You're just an old bear cat.

You made me feel so mean
You made me moan and groan
You made me feel so mean
You made me moan and groan
But you ain't lookin' for no man
You're just looking for an old soup bone.

HOUND DOG

J. LEIBER
M. STROLLER

You ain't nothin' but a hound dog
Quit snoopin' 'round my door
You ain't nothin' but a hound dog
Quit snoopin' round my door
You can wag your tail, but I ain't g
feed you no more

You told me you was high class
But I could see through that
Yes, you told me you was high class
But I could see through that
And Daddy I know you ain't no rea
cool cat

You made me so blue
You made me weep and moan
You made me so blue
You made me weep and moan
'Cause you ain't lookin' for a woman
All you lookin' is for a home

K. C. LOVING

MIKE STOLLER
JERRY LEIBER

I'm goin' to Kansas City
Kansas City, here I come
I'm goin' to Kansas City
Kansas City here I come
They got a crazy way of lovin' there
And I'm gonna get me some

I'm gonna be standin' on the corner
Twelfth Street and Vine
I'm gonna be standin' on the corner
Twelfth Street and Vine
With my Kansas City baby
And a bottle of Kansas City wine

Well I might take a train
I might take a plane
But if I have to walk
I'm goin' to Kansas City
Kansas City here I come
They got a crazy way of lovin' there
And I'm gonna get me some

I'm goin' to pack my clothes
Leave at the crack of dawn
I'm goin' to pack my clothes
Leave at the crack of dawn
My old lady will be sleepin'
And she won't know where I've gone

'Cause if I stay with that woman
I know I'm gonna die
Gotta find a friendly baby
And that's the reason why
I'm goin' to Kansas City
Kansas City, here I come
They got a crazy way of lovin' there
And I'm gonna get me some

KANS
(Also know

Blues tempo

CHORUS

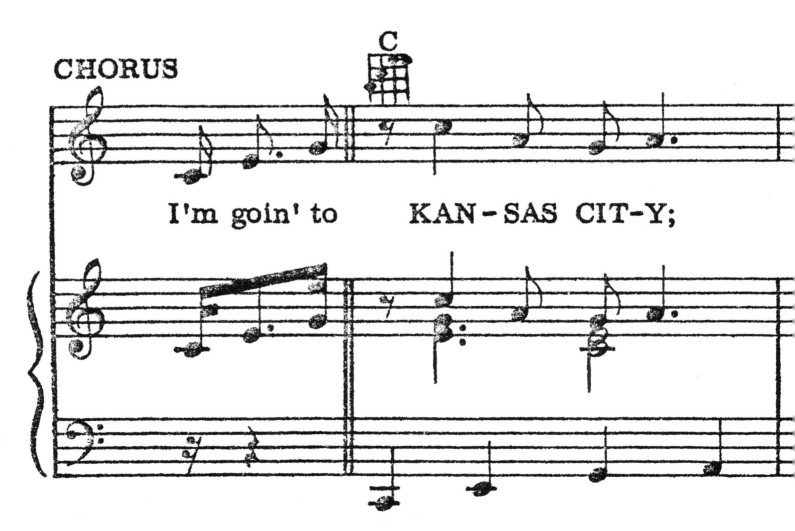

I'm goin' to   KAN-SAS CIT-Y;

C7   **F**

AS CITY
(as K. C. LOVING)

By MIKE STOLLER
and JERRY LEIBER

KAN-SAS CIT - Y, Here I come.

C

he Cash Box

50 ACROSS THE NATION

		Pos. Last Week
1	**KANSAS CITY** *Wilbert Harrison (Fury 1023)*	(2)

KANSAS CITY

I'm goin' to Kansas City, Kansas City, here I
 come
I'm goin' to Kansas City, Kansas City, here I
 come
They got a crazy way of lovin' there and I'm
 gonna get me some

I'm gonna be standin' on the corner, Twelfth
 Street and Vine
I'm gonna be standin' on the corner, Twelfth
 Street and Vine
With my Kansas City baby and a bottle of
 Kansas City wine

Well, I might take a train
I might take a plane
But if I have to walk
I'm goin' just the same
I'm goin' to Kansas City, Kansas City, here I
 come

They got a crazy way of lovin' there and I'm
 gonna get me some

I'm goin' to pack my clothes, leave at the
 crack of dawn
I'm goin' to pack my clothes, leave at the
 crack of dawn
My old lady will be sleepin' and she won't
 know where I'm gone

'Cause if I stay with that woman
I know I'm gonna die
Gotta find a brand-new baby
And that's the reason why
I'm goin' to Kansas City, Kansas City, here I
 come
They got a crazy way of lovin' there and I'm
 gonna get me some

Wilbert Harrison

Wynonie Harris

If the front tire blows I got a spare
If that one goes, I'll still get there
Destination love

James Brown

Well, I might take a train
I might take a plane
But if I have to walk
I'm goin' just the same
I'm goin' to Kansas City,
   Kansas City, here I come

La Vern Baker and King Curtis

You used to look so cute in your white sailor suit
Aboard that big white yacht that you no longer got
Don Juan, your money's gone
And when your money's gone, your baby's gone

The Isley Brothers

Mama, there's gonna be a dance tonight
Teach me how to dance real quick
Mama, if I don't know how to do it right
Chico's gonna steal my chick
Teach me how to shimmy
Like you and daddy do
Teach me how to shimmy
So I can shimmy, too

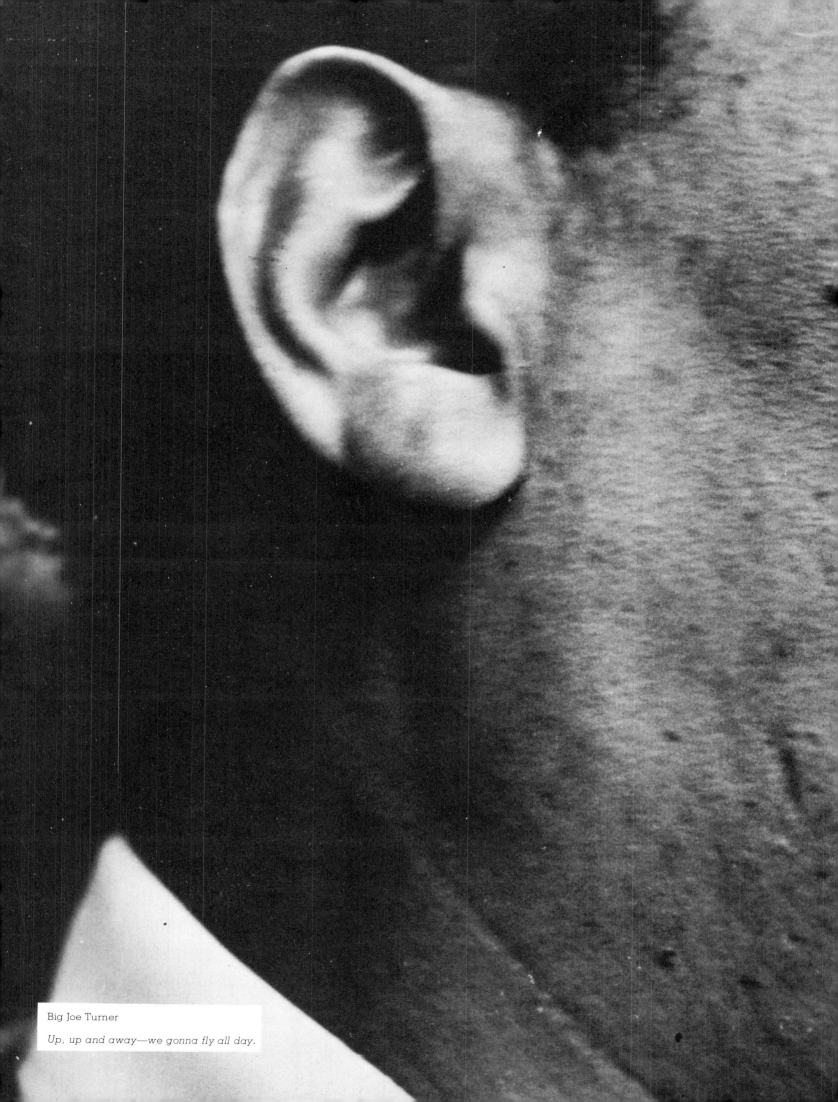

Big Joe Turner

Up, up and away—we gonna fly all day.

Little Esther

*I got a real fine station
And there's lots of trains in sight
But I want you to be my
Midnight Special tonight*

Charles Brown

*Blues have got me every day, every night
Hard times, ooh, I feel so bad
When I lost my baby, I lost everything I had*

Bull Moose Jackson

*There's a man in town all the women know
He goes by the name of Nosey Joe*

Back row, The Robins: (left to right) Billy Richards, Carl Gardner, Bobby Nunn, Roy Richards, and Ty Terrell. Front row, Anna Maria Alberghetti (first person), Gloria Haley Bregman (third), Perry Botkin, Jr., (sixth), Bert Convy (of The Cheers) (next), Buddy Bregman (arranger) (eighth), Jack Haley, Jr., (last).

Hank Ballard

I'm going to Kansas City
Gonna have myself some fun

Little Richard

*They got some pretty little foxes there
And I'm gonna get me one*

Ray Charles

Snow is fallin', fallin' on the cold, cold ground
Gloom and misery, gloom and misery all around

Linda Hopkins

When I shot him in the parlor
He fell down on the floor
That's one double-crossin' monkey
Ain't gonna swing no more

Dion DiMucci

I love a girl and Ruby is her name
She don't love me but I love her just the same
From the very day I metcha
Made a bet that I would getcha
Ruby, Ruby, when will you be mine?

Chuck Jackson

But these stupid old feet just head for your street
Like they've done so many times before
And this stubborn old fist on the end of my wrist
Starts knockin' on-a your front door
I keep forgettin' you don't love me no more

Jimmy Witherspoon

Well, she wasn't built for power
She wasn't built for speed
But she was built for comfort
And, Lord, that's what I need

Black Denim Trousers And Motorcycle Boots

Words and Music by MIKE STOLLER and JERRY LEIBER

RECORDED SUCCESSFULLY BY THE CHEERS AND LES BAXTER—CAPITOL No. 3219

The Cheers (left to right): Bert Convy, Sue Allen, Gil Garfield.

BLACK DENIM TROUSERS AND MOTORCYCLE BOOTS

He wore black denim trousers and motorcycle
   boots
And a black leather jacket with an eagle on
   the back
He had a hopped up 'cycle that took off like a
   gun
That fool was the terror of Highway 101

Well, he never washed his face and he never
   combed his hair
He had axle grease imbedded underneath his
   fingernails
On the muscle of his arm was a red tattoo,
A picture of a heart sayin', "Mother, I love
   you"

He had a pretty girlfriend by the name of
   Mary Lou
But he treated her just like he treated all the
   rest
And ev'rybody pitied her 'cause ev'rybody
   knew
He loved that doggone motorcycle best

He wore black denim trousers and motorcycle
   boots
And a black leather jacket with an eagle on
   the back

He had a hopped up 'cycle that took off like a
   gun
That fool was the terror of Highway 101

Mary Lou, poor girl, she pleaded and she
   begged him not to leave
She said, "I've got a feelin' if you ride tonight
   I'll grieve."
But her tears were shed in vain and her ev'ry
   word was lost
In the rumble of his engine and the smoke
   from his exhaust

He took off like a devil, there was fire in his
   eyes
He said, "I'll go a thousand miles before the
   sun can rise."
But he hit a screamin' Diesel that was
   California bound
And when they cleared the wreckage all they
   found

Was his black denim trousers and motorcycle
   boots
And a black leather jacket with an eagle on
   the back
But they couldn't find the 'cycle that took off
   like a gun
And they never found the terror of Highway
   101

L'HOMME A
LA MOTO
(BLACK DENIM TROUSERS AND MOTORCYCLE BOOTS)
une création de
musique de
MIKE STOLLER et JERRY LEIBER
Paroles Françaises de
JEAN DRÉJAC
EDITH PIAF
EDITIONS PIGALLE
67 rue de Provence
PARIS
"Columbia" SCRS. 197

*And when they cleared the wreckage all they found
Was his black denim trousers and motorcycle boots*

RIOT IN CELL BLOCK #9

On July the second, nineteen-fifty-three
I was servin' time for armed robbery
At four o'clock in the mornin' I was sleepin' in
   my cell
I heard a whistle blow then I heard somebody
   yell
There's a riot goin' on
There's a riot goin' on
There's a riot goin' on up in cell block #9

The trouble started in cell block #4
It spread like fire across the prison floor
I said, "O.K. boys get ready to run
Here come the warden, with a tommy gun"
There's a riot goin' on
There's a riot goin' on
There's a riot goin' on up in cell block #9

The warden said, "Come out with your hands
   up in the air
If you don't stop this riot, you're all gonna get
   the chair."
Scarface Jones said, "It's too late to quit
Pass the dynamite, cause the . . . fuse is lit"
There's a riot goin' on
There's a riot goin' on
There's a riot goin' on up in cell block #9

In the forty-seventh hour, the tear gas got our
   men
We're all back in our cells, but every now
   and then,
There's a riot goin' on
There's a riot goin' on
There's a riot goin' on up in cell block #9

PARK
RECORD CO.

IOT
IL BLOCK #9"

DOWN IN MEXICO

Down in Mexicali
There's a crazy little place that I know
Where the drinks are hotter than the chili
   sauce
And the boss is a cat named Joe
He wears a red bandana
Plays a blues piana
In a honky tonk down in Mexico
He wears a purple sash
And a black mustache
In a honky tonk down in Mexico

Well, the first time that I saw him
He was a-sittin' on a piano stool
I said, "Tell me, dad when does the fun
   begin?"
He just a-winked his eye and said, "Man be
   cool."
He wears a red bandana
Plays a blues piana
In a honky tonk down in Mexico
He wears a purple sash
And a black mustache
In a honky tonk down in Mexico

All of a sudden in walked a chick
Joe started playin' on a Latin kick
Around her waist she wore three fishnets
She started dancin' with her castanets
I didn't know just what to expect
She threw her arms around my neck
We started dancin' all around the floor
And then she did a dance I never saw before

So if you're south of the border
I mean a down in Mexico
And you wanna get straight, man don't
   hesitate
Just look up a cat named Joe
He wears a red bandana
Plays a blues piana
In a honky tonk down in Mexico
He wears a purple sash
And a black mustache
In a honky tonk down in Mexico

SEARCHIN'

I been searchin'
Searchin'—
Searchin' every which a-way

Oh, yes, I been searchin'
Searchin'
Searchin' every which a-way
But I'm like that Northwest Mountie
You know I'll bring her in some day

Well, now, if I have to swim a river, you
   know I will
And if I have to climb a mountain, you know I
   will
And if she's hidin' up on Blueberry Hill
Am I gonna find her, child, you know I will

'Cause I been searchin'
Searchin'—oh yeah
Searchin' every which a-way
But I'm like that Northwest Mountie
You know I'll bring her in some day

Well, Sherlock Holmes, Sam Spade, got
   nothin', child, on me
Sergeant Friday, Charlie Chan and Boston
   Blackie
No matter where she's hidin' she's gonna
   hear me comin'
I'm gonna walk right down that street like
   Bulldog Drummon'

'Cause I been searchin'
Searchin'—oh yeah
Searchin' every which a-way
But I'm like that Northwest Mountie
You know I'll bring her in some day

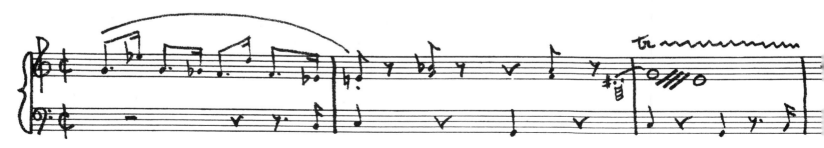

The Coasters, circa 1956. Standing (left to right) Carl Gardner, Bobby Nunn, Billy Guy. Kneeling, Leon Hughes.

The Coasters, circa 1958, at a recording session for Atlantic Records at 234 W. 56th Street, New York City. Above, from left to right: Billy Guy (baritone), "Dub" Jones (bass), Carl Gardner (tenor), Cornell Gunter (high tenor and falsetto), and Adolph Jacobs (guitarist). Right, Stoller and Leiber.

Tommy Dowd

Lester Sill

Leiber and Stoller with The Coasters and, from left to right, Lester Sill, manager of The Coasters, Jerry Wexler, executive at Atlantic Records, and, far right, Ahmet Ertegun

YAKETY YAK

Take out the papers and the trash
Or you don't get no spendin' cash
If you don't scrub that kitchen floor
You ain't gonna rock 'n roll no more

Yakety Yak

Don't talk back

Just finish cleanin' up your room
Let's see that dust fly with that broom
Get all that garbage out of sight
Or you don't go out Friday night

Yakety Yak

Don't talk back

You just put on your coat and hat
And walk yourself to the laundromat
And when you finish doin' that
Bring in the dog and put out the cat

Yakety Yak

Don't talk back

Don't you give me no dirty looks
Your father's hip, he knows what cooks
Just tell your hoodlum friends outside
You ain't got time to take a ride

Yakety Yak

Don't talk back

The Coasters receiving their second gold record—this time for "Yakety Yak."

Billy Guy and Carl Gardner goofing it up.

CHARLIE BROWN

Fee fee fi fi fo fo fum
I smell smoke in the auditorium.
Charlie Brown
Charlie Brown
He's a clown
That Charlie Brown
He's gonna get caught
Just you wait and see
"Why is everybody always pickin' on me?"

That's him on his knees, I know that's him
Yellin, "Seven come eleven" down in the
   boys' gym.
Charlie Brown
Charlie Brown
He's a clown
That Charlie Brown
He's gonna get caught
Just you wait and see
"Why is everybody always pickin' on me?"

Who's always writin' on the walls?
Who's always goofin' in the halls?
Who's always throwin' spitballs?
Guess who
Who me?
Yeah, you!

Who walks in the classroom cool and slow?
Who calls the English teacher "Daddy-O"?
Charlie Brown
Charlie Brown
He's a clown
That Charlie Brown
He's gonna get caught
Just you wait and see
"Why is everybody always pickin' on me?"

Cornell Gunter in "drag" with The Coasters at the Apollo.

LITTLE EGYPT

*Step right up folks and see Little Egypt do her
famous dance of the pyramids!*
She walks!
She talks!
She crawls on her belly like a reptile!
Just one thin dime,
One tenth of a dollar
Step right up folks!

I went and bought myself a ticket and I sat
down in the very first row
They pulled the curtain up and when they
turned the spotlight way down low
Little Egypt came out struttin' wearin' nuttin'
but a button and a bow
Singin', "Ying-yang, ying-yang
"Ying-yang, ying-yang"

She had a ruby on her tummy and a
diamond big as Texas on her toe
She let hair down and she did the hootchy-
kootchy real slow
When she did her special number on a zebra
skin I thought they'd stop the show
Singin', "Ying-yang, ying-yang
"Ying-yang, ying-yang"

She did a triple somersault an' when she hit
the ground
she winked at the audience an' then she
turned around
She had a picture of a cowoboy tattooed on
her spine
Sayin', "Phoenix, Arizona, 1949"

Yeah, but let me tell you people Little Egypt
doesn't dance there anymo'
She's too busy mopping and a-taking care of
shopping at the sto'
'Cause we got seven kids and all day long
they crawl around the flo'
Singin', "Ying-yang, ying-yang
"Ying-yang, ying-yang"

ALONG CAME JONES

I plopped down in my easy chair and turned
   on Channel Two
A bad gun slinger called Salty Sam was
   a-chasin' poor Sweet Sue
He trapped her in the old saw mill an' said
   with an evil laugh,
"If you don't gimme the deed to your ranch I'll
   saw you-all in half."
And then he grabbed her.
And then?
He tied her up.
And then?
He turned on the buzz saw.
And then, and then?

And then along came Jones
Tall thin Jones
Slow walkin' Jones
Slow talkin' Jones
Along came long, lean, lanky Jones.

The commercial came on so I got up to get
   myself a snack
You should have seen what was goin' on by
   the time that I got back
Down in the old abandoned mine Sweet Sue
   was a-havin' fits
That villain said, "Gimme the deed to your
   ranch or I'll blow you-all to bits."
And then he grabbed her.
And then?
He tied her up.
And then?
He lit the fuse to the dynamite.
And then, and then?

And then along came Jones
Tall thin Jones
Slow walkin' Jones
Slow talkin' Jones
Along came long, lean, lanky Jones.

I got so bugged I turned it off an' turned on
   another show
But there was the same old shoot-'em-up and
   the same old rodeo
Salty Sam was tryin' to stuff Sweet Sue in a
   burlap sack

He said, "If you don't gimme the deed to your
   ranch I'm gonna throw you on the railroad
   track."

And then he grabbed her.
And then?
He tied her up.
And then?
He threw her on the railroad track.
And then?
A train started comin'.
And then, and then, and then? . . .

And then along came Jones
Tall thin Jones
Slow walkin' Jones
Slow talkin' Jones
Along came long, lean, lanky Jones.

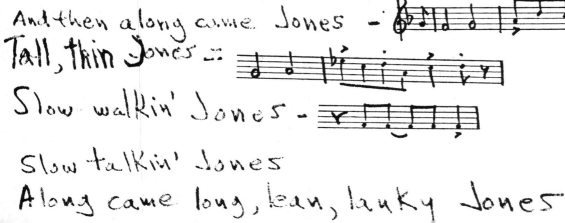

And then along came Jones –
Tall, thin Jones –
Slow walkin' Jones –
Slow talkin' Jones
Along came long, lean, lanky Jones

ALONG CAME JONES

Words and Music by JERRY LEIBER and MIKE STOLLER

Young Blood

Verse - Moderato With A Rock

1. I saw her stand-ing on the cor-ner ___
2. I took one look and I was frac-tured ___

A yel-low rib-bon in her hair, I could-n't keep my-self from
I tried to walk but I was lame, I tried to talk but I just

shout-ing ___ "Look-a there, *Spoken* look-a there, look-a there, look-a there!"
stut-tered ___ "What's your name, what's your name, what's your name, what's your name?"

Refrain

YOUNG BLOOD   YOUNG BLOOD   YOUNG BLOOD

POISON IVY

Young Jessie

POISON IVY

She comes on like a rose
But everybody knows
She'll get you in dutch
You can look but you better not touch

Poison Ivy, Poison Ivy
Late at night while you're sleepin'
Poison Ivy comes a-creepin' around.

She's pretty as a daisy
But look out, man, she's crazy
She'll really do you in
If you let her get under your skin

Poison Ivy, Poison Ivy
Late at night while you're sleepin'
Poison Ivy comes a-creepin' around.

Measles make you bumpy
And mumps'll make you lumpy
And chicken pox'll make you jump and
    twitch.
A common cold'll fool ya
And whoopin' cough can cool ya
But Poison Ivy, Lawd, will make you itch.

You're gonna need an ocean
Of Calamine lotion
You'll be scratchin' like a hound
The minute you start to mess around

Poison Ivy, Poison Ivy
Late at night while you're sleepin'
Poison Ivy comes a-creepin' around.

RUN RED RUN

Ol' Red went and bought himself a monkey
He got him from a pawnshop broker
He taught that monkey how to guzzle beer
And he taught him how to play stud poker
Last night they was gamblin' in the kitchen
An' the monkey, he was takin' a beatin'
The monkey said, "Red, I'm gonna shoot you
     dead
Because I know darn well you been cheatin' "

Run, Red, run, 'cause he's got your gun
And he's aimin' it at your head
Run, Red, run, 'cause he's got your gun
And he's aimin' it at your head
You better get up and wail
You better move your tail
Before he fills it full of lead

Ol' Red jumped up an' he started to move
Like a P-80 Saber jet
He zoomed around the corner an' he
     disappeared
An' ev'rybody started to bet
The race was on, you know the chase was on
That Red, he sure could run
But, let me tell you, sport, don't sell that
     monkey short,
'Cause he's a travellin' son-of-a-gun

Run, Red, run, 'cause he's got your gun
And he's aimin' it at your head
Run, Red, run, 'cause he's got your gun
And he's aimin' it at your head
You better get up and wail
You better move your tail
Before he fills it full of lead

The monkey trapped Red in a parkin' lot
Down along the avenue
The monkey said, "Red, you made a man out
     of me
Now I'm gonna make a monkey out of you."
He said, "Gimme your car keys an' gimme
     your watch
Hand 'em over or else I'll shoot
I'm gonna put on your brand new Stetson hat
An' go to town in your new brown suit"

Run, Red, run, 'cause he's got your gun
And he's aimin' it at your head
Run, Red, run, 'cause he's got your gun
And he's aimin' it at your head
You better get up and wail
You better move your tail
Before he fills it full of lead

THE SHADOW KNOWS

You can hide down in the alley
With your hat pulled over your eyes
You can wear a wig or mustache
Or any old disguise
You can change your name an' address
You can change your style of clothes
Even change your style of clothes
But the shadow knows
The shadow knows

You thought you had me baffled
You thought I didn't know
But I know where you're goin', baby,
Long before you go
You can't even snap your fingers
Or wiggle your toes
Without the shadow knows
The shadow knows

Now baby, stop your jivin'
And your messin' 'round
Because I know what you're puttin'
Long before you put it down
You better mind your P's and Q's
And your M's an' N's an' O's
Because the shadow knows
The shadow knows

DOWN HOME GIRL

Words by Jerry Leiber
Music by Artie Butler

Lord, I swear the perfume you wear smell like
 turnip greens
An' every time I kiss you, chile, it taste like
 pork and beans
'N even though you're wearin' those cityfied
 high heels
I can tell by your giant step you been walkin'
 through them cotton fields

Oh,
You're so
Down home girl

Your shoes are green, your dress is red and
 your wig hat is powder blue
But underneath all that mess is the same old
 stinky you
You're sittin' there in that fancy chair, drinkin'
 champagne like a movie star
When you oughta be sittin' on a curbstone,
 sippin' white lightenin' out of a jelly jar

Oh,
You're so
Down home girl

You say you don't eat pig meat, baby, but I
 know that ain't for real
I seen you at the barbecue and you ate up
 everything but the squeal
You tell me you from New York, baby, but I
 know you from way down south
'Cause I can hear the Mississippi, momma,
 every time you open your mouth

Oh,
You're so
Down home girl

THAT IS ROCK N' ROLL

In the beginning there was nothing but rocks
Then somebody invented the wheel
And things just began to roll

Did you ever hear a tenor sax
Swingin' like a rusty axe
Honkin' like a frog
Down in a hollow log
Baby, that is rock n' roll

Did you ever hear a guitar twang
Jingy jingy jingy jang
Ever hear those strings
Doin' crazy things
Baby, that is rock n' roll

That ain't no freight train that you hear
Rollin' down the railroad tracks
That's a country-born piano man
Playin' in between the cracks

You say that music's for the birds
And you can't understand the words
Well, honey, if you did
You'd really blow your lid
'Cause baby, that is rock n' roll

OF SUCCESS

Numéro 2   Samedi 8 Décembre 1962 - Paraît le Samedi   Prix : 0,50 NF

LE CLIMB
a pris naissance au Golf Drouot

Apprenez à danser LE CLIMB

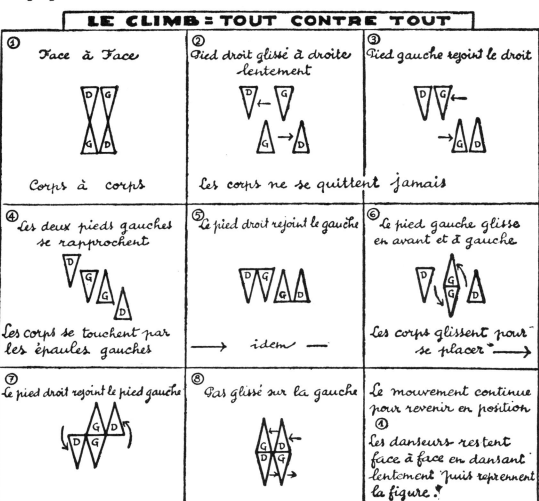

LE CLIMB = TOUT CONTRE TOUT

① Face à Face

Corps à corps

② Pied droit glissé à droite lentement

③ Pied gauche rejoint le droit

Les corps ne se quittent jamais

④ Les deux pieds gauches se rapprochent

Les corps se touchent par les épaules gauches

⑤ Le pied droit rejoint le gauche

→ idem →

⑥ Le pied gauche glisse en avant et à gauche

Les corps glissent pour se placer →

⑦ Le pied droit rejoint le pied gauche

→ lentement →

⑧ Pas glissé sur la gauche

dos à dos

Le mouvement continue pour revenir en position ①
Les danseurs restent face à face en dansant lentement puis reprennent la figure !

"The Climb" (originally titled "The Slime") was a spoof of the dance crazes of the day: The Slop, The Mashed Potato, etc. Left, dance instructions.

D.W. WASHBURN

"D.W. Washburn," I heard a sweet voice say.
"D.W. Washburn, this is your lucky day.
A hot bowl of soup is waitin'—
A hot bowl of soup an' a shave.
D.W. Washburn, we picked you to save."

"Can't you hear the flugelhorn?
Can't you hear the bell?
Even you can be reborn,
You naughty ne'er-do-well
If you don't get outta that gutter
Before the next big rain,
D.W. Washburn, you're gonna wash right
    down the drain."

"Up! Up! C'mon get up!
Get up off the street.
If you can only make it to your hands and
    knees,
I know you can make it to your feet."

"D.W. Washburn," I said to myself,
"D.W. Washburn, why don't they go save
    somebody else?"
You see, I got no job to go to
Don't work, and I don't get paid
I got a bottle of wine and I'm feelin' fine
And I believe I've got it made.

I'd like to thank all you good people
For comin' to my aid,
But I'm D.W. Washburn
And I believe I've got it made.

THE SLIME

Cheek to cheek
Toes to toes
Here's a dance you can do on a dime.
Knees to knees
Nose to nose
Hardly move and you're doin' The Slime.

Heart to heart
Soul to soul
Shake that thing, baby, till it's a crime.
Hips to hips
Let 'em roll
Hardly move and you're doin' The Slime

This ain't for fancy pants
Stuffed shirts or maiden aunts
This here's a down home dance for down
    home folks!

Round an' round
Side to side
When you slime, you don't have to keep time.
Let your feet
Slowly slide
Hardly move and you're doin' The . . .
    squatty-watty-doo.
Hardly move and you're doin' The . . .
    squatty-watty.
Hardly move and you're doin' The . . . squat.
Hardly move and you're doin' The . . . Slime.

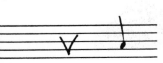

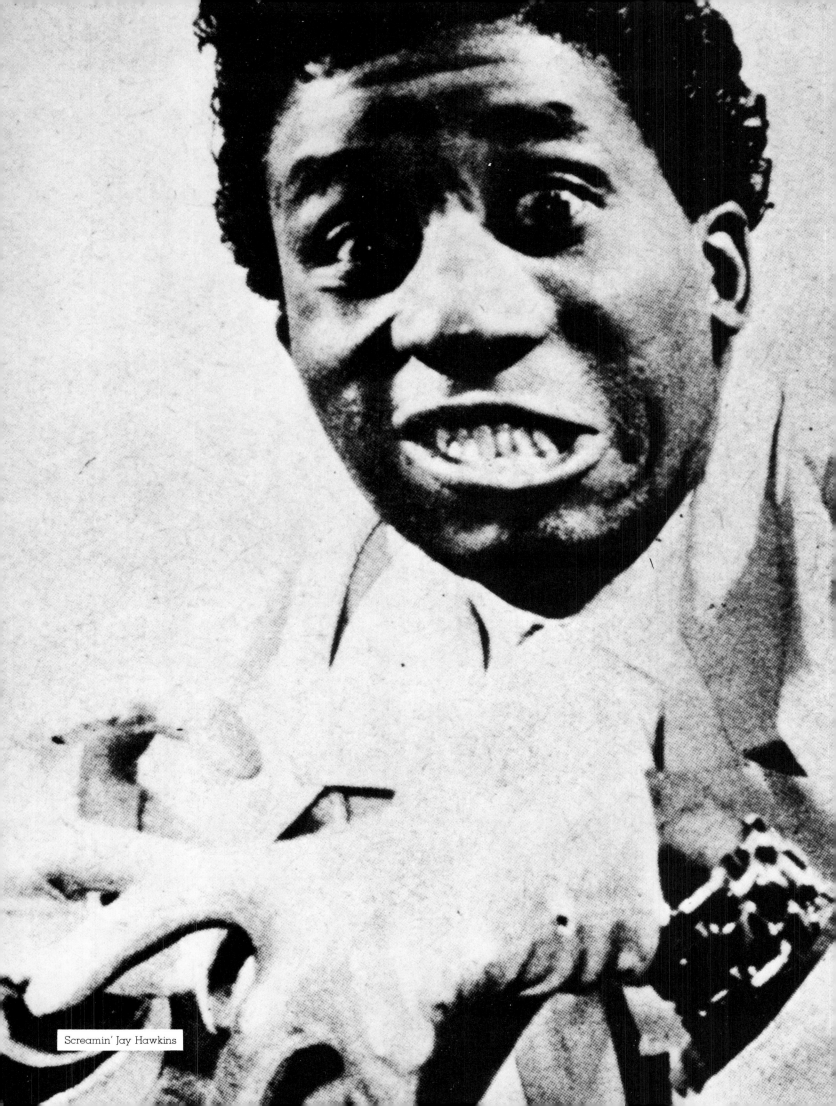

Screamin' Jay Hawkins

ALLIGATOR WINE

Take the blood out of an alligator
Take the left eye out of a fish
Take the skin off of a frog
And mix it all up in a dish
Add a cup of green swamp water
Then count from one to nine
Spit over your left shoulder
You got alligator wine

Alligator wine,
You old porcupine,
Is gonna make you mine.

It'll make your head boil, baby
It'll make your big toe freeze
It'll turn your blood right into steam
It'll make you cough and sneeze
You gonna scream like a big bald eagle

You gonna roar like a mountain lion
When you get finished drinkin'
My alligator wine

Alligator wine,
You old porcupine,
Is gonna make you mine.

Meet me at the stroke of midnight
By the swamp down in the wood
I'm gonna make you love me
Like you never thought you could
When you drink my magic potion
Your bloodshot eyes will shine
And you'll be a slave forever
To my alligator wine

Alligator wine,
You old porcupine,
Is gonna make you mine.

I (WHO HAVE NOTHING)

I, I who have nothing
I, I who have no one
Adore you and want you so
I'm just a no one,
With nothing to give you but, oh,
I love you

He, he buys you diamonds
Bright, sparkling diamonds
But believe me, dear, when I say
That he can give you the world
But he'll never love you the way
I love you

He can take you any place he wants
To fancy clubs and restaurants
Where I can only watch you with
My nose pressed up against the window pane

I, I who have nothing
I, I who have no one
Must watch you go dancing by
Wrapped in the arms of somebody else
When darling it's I
Who love you.

Ben E. King

90

Aretha Franklin

SPANISH HARLEM
by Jerry Leiber and Phil Spector

There is a rose in Spanish Harlem
A red rose up in Spanish Harlem
It is a special one
It's never seen the sun
It only comes out when the moon is on the run
And all the stars are gleaming
It's growing in the street
Right up through the concrete
But soft and sweet
And dreaming
There is a rose in Spanish Harlem
A red rose up in Spanish Harlem
With eyes as black as coal
That look down in my soul
And start a fire there and then I lose control
I'll have to beg your pardon
I'm going to pick that rose
And watch her as she grows
In my garden

91

SAVED

I used to smoke
I used to drink
I used to smoke
Drink
And play the numbers, too
I used to smoke and drink
Smoke and drink and play the numbers, too
But now I'm standin' on this corner
Prayin' for me and you

Because I'm saved . . . saved
People let me tell you 'bout kingdom come
You know I'm saved . . . saved
I can preach until you're deaf and dumb
I'm in that soul-savin' army
Beatin' on the big bass drum

I used to cuss
I used to fuss
I used to cuss
Fuss
And boogie all night long
I used to cuss and fuss
Cuss and fuss and boogie all night long
But now I'm standin' on this corner
I know right from wrong.

Because I'm saved . . . saved
People let me tell you 'bout kingdom come
You know I'm saved . . . saved
I can preach until you're deaf and dumb
I'm in that soul-savin' army
Beatin' on the big bass drum

I used to lie
I used to cheat
I used to lie
Cheat
And step on people's feet
I used to lie and cheat
Lie and cheat and step on people's feet
But now I'm steppin' on to glory
Salvation is my beat

Because I'm saved . . . saved
People let me tell you 'bout kingdom come
You know I'm saved . . . saved
I can preach until you're deaf and dumb
I'm in that soul-savin' army
Beatin' on the big bass drum

La Vern Baker

Ruth Brown

*When I was just a little thing
With long and silky curls
My mama told me, "Honey,
You've got more than other girls"*

DON JUAN

Don Juan, your money's gone
And when your money's gone, Don, your
    baby's gone
Don Juan, your baby's gone
Stiff upper lip now, Don, you'll have to
    carry on

The house we moved in
The house we grooved in
The way we waltzed around those marble
    floors
You sure did look deluxe
In your white tie and tux
Up in that big white house that is no longer
    yours

Don Juan, your money's gone
And when your money's gone, Don, your
    baby's gone
Don Juan, your baby's gone
Stiff upper lip now, Don, you'll have to
    carry on

The yacht we sailed on,
The yacht we wailed on
I got to tell you, Don, I loved that yacht
You used to look so cute
In your white sailor suit
Aboard that big white yacht that you no
    longer got

Don Juan, your money's gone
And when your money's gone, Don, your
    baby's gone
Don Juan, your baby's gone
Stiff upper lip now, Don, you'll have to
    carry on

        Don Juan, when you had money
        Don Juan, I was your honey
        But Don, it's gone, and so am I

The jet we cruised on
The jet we boozed on
That was the highest I have ever flown
You swept me off my feet
At forty thousand feet
Up in that big white jet that you no longer
    own

Don Juan, your money's gone
And when your money's gone, Don, your
    baby's gone
Don Juan, your baby's gone
Stiff upper lip now, Don, you'll have to
    carry on

LOVE POTION #9

I took my troubles down to Madame Ruth
You know that gypsy with the gold-capped
   tooth
She's got a storefront at Thirty-fourth and Vine
Sellin' little bottles of Love Potion #9

I told her that I was a flop with chicks
"I been this way since 1956"
She looked at my palm and she made a
   magic sign
She said, "What you need is Love Potion #9"

She bent down, turned around and gave me
   a wink
She said, "I'm gonna mix it up right here in
   the sink."
It smelled like turpentine and looked like India
   ink
I held my nose, I closed my eyes, I took a
   drink

I didn't know if it was day or night
I started kissin' everything in sight
But when I kissed the cop down at Thirty-
   fourth and Vine
He broke my little bottle of Love Potion #9

The Clovers

The Drifters, circa 1963: Left to right, Charlie Thomas, "Doc" Green, Tommy Evans (seated), Rudy Lewis. Below, The Drifters, 1959: (left to right) Charlie Thomas, Ben E. King, "Doc" Green, Ellsbury Hobbs.

ON BROADWAY

They say the neon lights are bright—on
　　Broadway
They say there's always magic in the air.
But when you're walkin' down that street
And you ain't had enough to eat
The glitter rubs right off and you're
　　nowhere—on Broadway

They say the girls are somethin' else—on
　　Broadway
But lookin' at them just gives me the blues
'Cause how ya gonna make some time
When all you got is one thin dime
And one thin dime won't even shine your
　　shoes—on Broadway

They say that I won't last too long—on
　　Broadway
I'll catch a Greyhound bus for home, they say
But they're dead wrong, I know they are
'Cause I can play this here guitar
And I won't quit till I'm a star—on Broadway

Mike Stoller, Elvis Presley, and Jerry Leiber.

Elvis sings ''Hound Dog'' on Steve Allen's TV show.

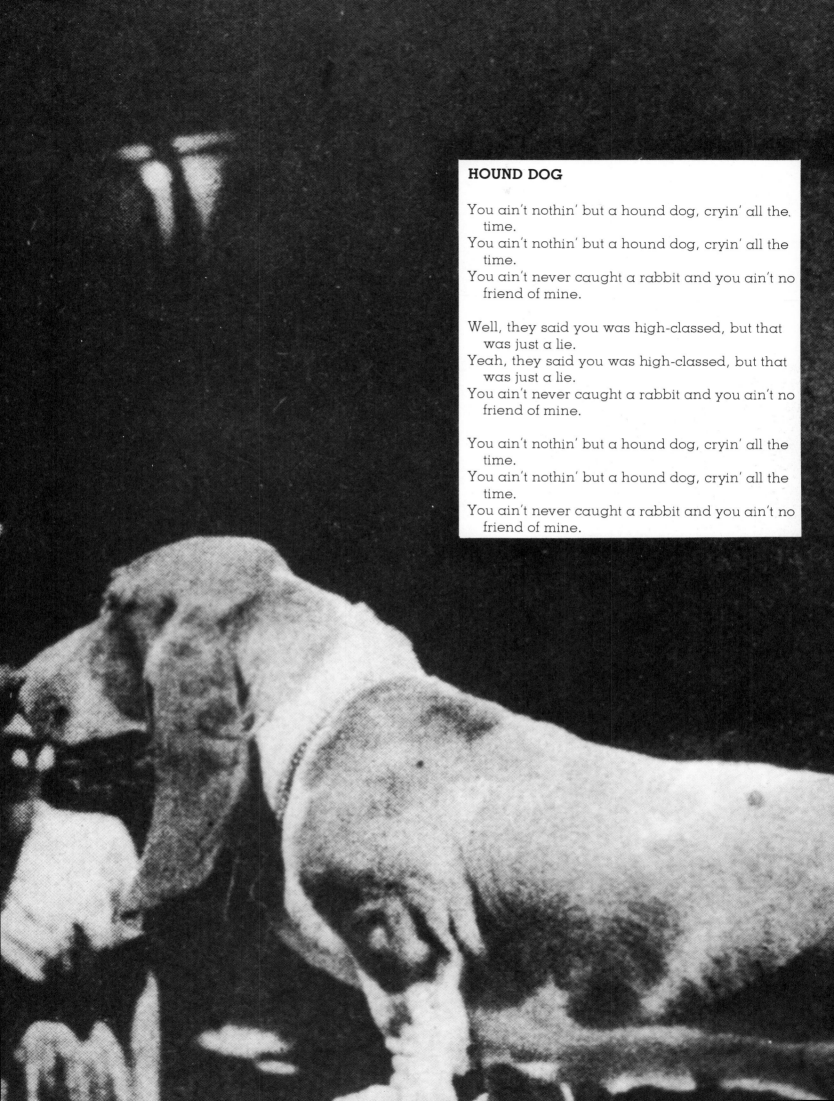

HOUND DOG

You ain't nothin' but a hound dog, cryin' all the
   time.
You ain't nothin' but a hound dog, cryin' all the
   time.
You ain't never caught a rabbit and you ain't no
   friend of mine.

Well, they said you was high-classed, but that
   was just a lie.
Yeah, they said you was high-classed, but that
   was just a lie.
You ain't never caught a rabbit and you ain't no
   friend of mine.

You ain't nothin' but a hound dog, cryin' all the
   time.
You ain't nothin' but a hound dog, cryin' all the
   time.
You ain't never caught a rabbit and you ain't no
   friend of mine.

DON'T

Don't, don't, that's what you say
Each time that I hold you this way.
When I feel like this and I want to kiss you
Baby don't say don't.

Don't, don't leave my embrace,
For here in my arms is your place.
When the night grows cold and I want to hold
    you
Baby, don't say don't.

If you think that this is just a game I'm
    playing,
If you think that I don't mean every word I'm
    saying

Don't, don't, don't feel that way
I'm your love and yours I will stay.
This you can believe; I will never leave you
Heaven knows I won't
Baby, don't say don't.

LOVE ME

Treat me like a fool,
Treat me mean and cruel,
But love me.
Break my faithful heart,
Tear it all apart,
But love me.

If you ever go,
Darling, I'll be oh
So lonely.
I'll be sad and blue,
Crying over you,
Dear, only.

> I would beg and steal
> Just to feel
> Your heart beating close to mine

Every night I pray
To the stars that shine
Above me,
Begging on my knees,
All I ask is please,
Please love me.

TREAT ME NICE

When I walk through that door, baby, be polite.
You're gonna make me sore if you don't
 greet me right.
Don'tcha ever kiss me once, kiss me twice.
Treat me nice.

I know that you've been told it's not fair to tease
So if you come on cold, I'm really gonna freeze.
If you don't want me to be cold as ice,
Treat me nice.

Make me feel at home
If you really care.
Scratch my back and run
 your pretty fingers through my hair

You know I'd be your slave if you ask me to.
But if you don't behave, I'll walk right out on you.
If you want my love then take my advice.
Treat me nice.

(YOU'RE SO SQUARE) BABY, I DON'T CARE

You don't like crazy music
You don't like rockin' bands
You just wanna go to a movie show
And sit there holdin' hands
You're so square
Baby, I don't care

You don't like hot rod racin'
Or drivin' late at night
You just wanna park where it's nice and dark
You just wanna hold me tight
You're so square
Baby, I don't care

You don't know any dance steps that are new
But no one else can love me like you do

I don't know why my heart flips
I only know it does
I wonder why I love you, babe
I guess it's just becuz
You're so square
Baby, I don't care

JAILHOUSE ROCK — JAILHOUSE ROCK — JAILHOUSE ROCK
KODAK SAFETY FILM 5063

A still from the film *Jailhouse Rock* (1957): left to right, Mike Stoller (in roll of piano player), Elvis Presley, Scotty Moore (Elvis's guitar player), Judy Tyler, Bill Black (Elvis's bass player), Mickey Shaughnessy, D.J. Fontana (Elvis's drummer).

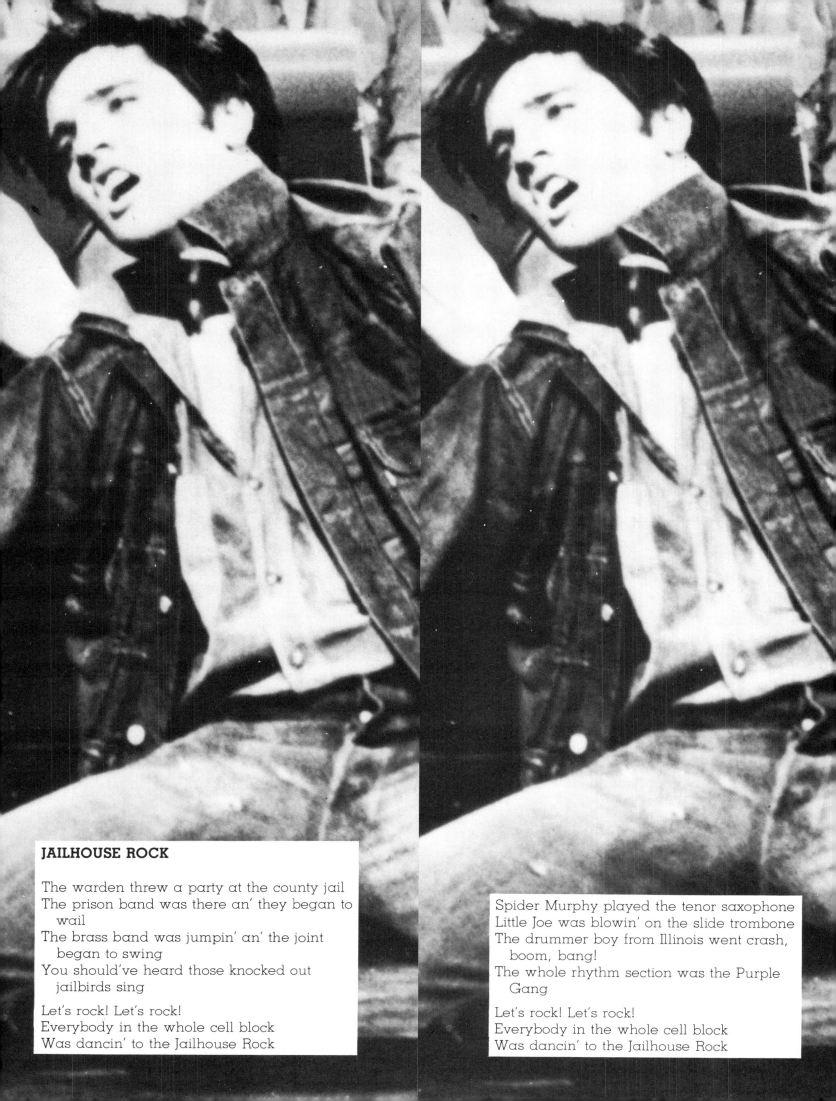

JAILHOUSE ROCK

The warden threw a party at the county jail
The prison band was there an' they began to
    wail
The brass band was jumpin' an' the joint
    began to swing
You should've heard those knocked out
    jailbirds sing

Let's rock! Let's rock!
Everybody in the whole cell block
Was dancin' to the Jailhouse Rock

Spider Murphy played the tenor saxophone
Little Joe was blowin' on the slide trombone
The drummer boy from Illinois went crash,
    boom, bang!
The whole rhythm section was the Purple
    Gang

Let's rock! Let's rock!
Everybody in the whole cell block
Was dancin' to the Jailhouse Rock

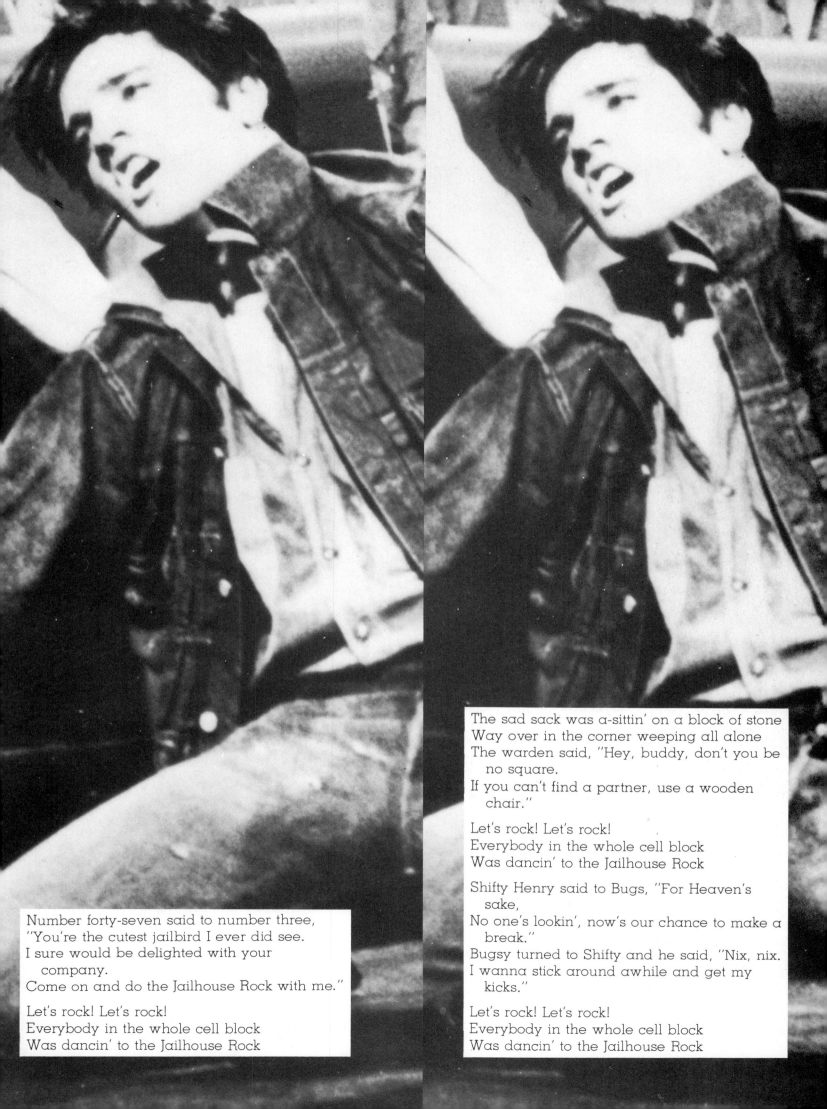

The sad sack was a-sittin' on a block of stone
Way over in the corner weeping all alone
The warden said, "Hey, buddy, don't you be
    no square.
If you can't find a partner, use a wooden
    chair."

Let's rock! Let's rock!
Everybody in the whole cell block
Was dancin' to the Jailhouse Rock

Shifty Henry said to Bugs, "For Heaven's
    sake,
No one's lookin', now's our chance to make a
    break."
Bugsy turned to Shifty and he said, "Nix, nix.
I wanna stick around awhile and get my
    kicks."

Let's rock! Let's rock!
Everybody in the whole cell block
Was dancin' to the Jailhouse Rock

Number forty-seven said to number three,
"You're the cutest jailbird I ever did see.
I sure would be delighted with your
    company.
Come on and do the Jailhouse Rock with me."

Let's rock! Let's rock!
Everybody in the whole cell block
Was dancin' to the Jailhouse Rock

HOUND DOG
LOVE ME
LOVING YOU
HOT DOG!
JAILHOUSE ROCK
RCA
47-7000
(H2WW-0418)
Elvis Presley Mus.
BMI
TREAT ME NICE
BABY, I DON'T CARE
I WANT TO BE FREE
DON'T
SANTA CLAUS IS BACK IN TOWN
TRADE MARKS • REGISTERED • MARCAS REGISTRADAS •
ELVIS
with

CTOR

45 R.P.M.
"NEW ORTHOPHONIC"
HIGH FIDELITY

JUST TELL HER JIM SAID HELLO
GIRLS, GIRLS, GIRLS
BOSSA NOVA BABY
FOOLS FALL IN LOVE
THREE CORN PATCHES

KING CREOLE
TROUBLE
STEADFAST, LOYAL AND TRUE
DIRTY, DIRTY FEELIN'
SHE'S NOT YOU

(oller)

RESLEY

rdanaires

CORPORATION OF AMERICA — CAMDEN, N. J.— MADE IN U.S.A.

ELVI "
TECHNICOLOR "
PRODUCTION

S PRESLEY
LOVING YOU

LOVING YOU

I will spend my whole life through
Loving you, loving you
Winter, summer, springtime, too
Loving you, loving you
Makes no difference where I go
Or what I do
You know that I'll always be
Loving you

If I'm seen with someone new
Don't be blue, don't be blue
I'll be faithful, I'll be true
Always true, true to you
There is only one for me
And you know who
You know that I'll always be
Loving you

I'M A WOMAN

Words and Music by
JERRY LEIBER and MIKE STOLLER

Recorded by
PEGGY LEE

on

TRIO MUSIC CO., INC.

06115

60

I'M A WOMAN

I can wash out forty-four pairs of socks an'
    have them hangin' out on the line,
I can starch an' iron two dozen shirts before
    you can count from one to nine,
I can scoop up a great big dipper full of lard
    from the drippin's can,
Throw it in the skillet, go out an' do my shoppin'
    an' be back before it melts in the pan,

'Cause I'm a woman
W—O—M—A—N
I'll say it again.

I can rub an' scrub till this old house is shinin'
    like a dime,
Feed the baby, grease the car an' powder my
    face at the same time,
Get all dressed up, go out an' swing till four
    a.m., and then
Lay down at five, jump up at six an' start all
    over again,

'Cause I'm a woman
W—O—M—A—N
I'll say it again.

If you come to me sickly, you know I'm gonna
    make you well.
If you come to me hexed up, you know I'm
    gonna break the spell.
If you come to me hungry, you know I'll fill
    you full o' grits.
If it's lovin' you're lackin', I'll kiss ya an' give
    ya the shiverin' fits,

'Cause I'm a woman
W—O—M—A—N
I'll say it again.

I can stretch a greenback dollar bill from here
    to kingdom come.
I can play the numbers, pay my bills, an' still
    end up with some.
I got a twenty dollar gold piece says there
    ain't nothin' I can't do.
I can make a dress out of a feed bag an' I can
    make a man out of you,

'Cause I'm a woman
W—O—M—A—N
I'll say it again.

Recordings of Works by Leiber and Stoller

(Includes compositions written by Jerry Leiber and/or Mike Stoller jointly, individually, and/or in conjunction with other writers.)
(The name "Elmo Glick" is a pseudonym for Jerry Leiber and Mike Stoller jointly.)

AFTER TAXES
(Leiber-Wheeler)
*Billy Edd Wheeler (1963) Kapp KS-3351. Also: Kapp (45) K550, (LP) 1351
Cab Calloway, (ABC Paramount) Boom 60006
Johnny Cash, CBS 35313

ALL IS WELL
ALLEY MUSIC
Joel Kaye
Chuck Kaye
(pseudonyms for Jerry Leiber and Mike Stoller)
Johnny Mathis (1960) Columbia 4-41583
*The Sly Fox (1955) Spark 112
(Vocal & Maracas: Jerry Leiber
Piano: Mike Stoller)

ALLIGATOR WINE
ALONG CAME JONES
Screamin' Jay Hawkins (1958) Okeh 4-7101
*The Coasters (1959) Atco (45) 6141. Also: (45) 13006, (33) 111, (33) 371, Trip TRP 1607
Dolenz, Jones, Boyce & Hart, Capitol ST 11513
Ray Stevens, Barnaby (45) 517, Also: (LP)5004 & 5010 Monument SLP 18115
Buck Owens, Pickwick, JS6128
Las Jerolas, (JONES S'EST MONTRE), RCA KSL2-0107
Henri Salvador (ZORRO EST ARRIVE) (F) (n/a)
Righteous Bros. Verve VK-10479 (45)

(YOU'RE SO SQUARE)
BABY, I DON'T CARE
Elvis Presley (1957) RCA EP 4114. Also: LP LSP2011
Mike Berry, Sire D-7524
Brian Ferry, Atco 7304
Buddy Holly, (n/a)

BACK DOOR BLUES
BAD BLOOD
Jimmy Witherspoon (1953) Federal 12138 (78)
*The Coasters (1961) Atco 6210 also LP 33-135
The Plebs, MGM 13320

BAZOOM (I NEED YOUR LOVIN')
*The Cheers (1954) Capitol 2921 (78). Also: Capitol (45) 6212, (LP) 1414
The Fleetwoods, Dolton BST 8011
*Leiber & Stoller Big Band, Atlantic 8047
The Charms, Deluxe 6076 (78)
Les Elgart, Columbia 40388 (78)
The Three Belles, Bell 1079

BEEN DOWN SO LONG
*Eddie James (1973) King 6413
*T-Bone Walker, Reprise 2XS6483
The Cheers (1955) Capitol 3019 (78)

BERNIE'S TUNE
Lyric: Leiber & Stoller
Music: Miller

BEST THING, THE
Leiber, Stoller, Dino, Sembello
*Dino & Sembello (1974) A&M SP3657
Billy Eckstine, A&M-1858
Philip & Vanessa, Anchor 2003

BLACK DENIM TROUSERS AND MOTORCYCLE BOOTS
The Cheers (1955) Capitol 3219. Also: 6212
Jack Brooks, Decca 29684
The Diamonds, Coral 61502
Eddie Mill, RCA Victor 47-6279
Ramblin' Jimmy Dolan, Capitol 3254
Edith Piaf (L'HOMME A LA MOTO) Capitol 3368 (45). Also: (LP) (Live) TB 22193, (F) Odeon SCX6477
*Leiber/Stoller Big Band, Atlantic 8047
Vaughan Monroe, RCA Victor 147-6260
Joan Morris & William Bolcom, Nonesuch H-71346

BLOOD IS REDDER THAN WINE
BLUEBERRIES
Little Willie Littlefield (1952) Federal 12101 (78)
The Cheers (1954) Capitol 3075

BLUES FOR ME
BOSSA NOVA BABY
Georgia Gibbs, Mercury 70647
Eddie Fisher (1957) RCA Victor 47-6849
*Tippie & the Clovers (1963) Tiger 201
Elvis Presley, RCA Victor (45) 447-0642. Also: (LP) LSP 2756, LPM 6401
Werner Muller cond. London Festival Orch., London SP44217

BOSSA NOVA (MY HEART SAID), THE
Leiber, Stoller, Mann & Weil
*Tippie & the Clovers (1963) Tiger 201
*Irene Reid, Verve VK 10286

BOYS IN THE BAND, THE
The Boys in the Band (1964) Spring 103
Glass Bottle, Avco Embassy AVE 33012

BROTHER BILL (THE LAST CLEAN SHIRT)
Leiber, Stoller, Otis
*The Honeyman (1965) Red Bird 10-007
*T-Bone Walker, Reprise 2XS6483
The Animals, Jet JTLA 790-M
Cactus, Atco 33-340
The Rockin Berries, Warner Bros. 3256

BULL DOG
BULL TICK WALTZ
CAFE ESPRESSO (instr.)
CANDLE'S BURNIN' LOW THE
*The Shangri-Las (1965) Red Bird 20-101
*The Coasters (1962) Atco 6251
*The Leiber-Stoller Orch. (1962) U.A. 441
Johnny Otis (1952) Mercury 8295 (78) (Voc. Mel Walker)

CAN'T WE BE MORE THAN FRIENDS
*The Cheers (1954) Capitol 3075

CASE OF M.J., THE (a.k.a. MARY JANE)
*Peggy Lee (1975) A&M SP4547

CHA! BULL! (THE CROWD)
*David Hill & His Men (1958) RCA Victor 47-7322
Bert Kaemfert, Polydor 23888

CHARLIE BROWN
*The Coasters (1959) Atco 6132. Also: (45) 13007, (LP) 33-371, Roulette LP 112, 4202S
Chet Atkins, RCA Victor, VPS 6030
Boots Randolph, Monument ML 6600. Also: MG7602
Lonnie Smith, Bluenote BLN 84326
Melvin Sparks, Prestige PRS 10001
James Last, Polydor 2634052
Compton Bros., Dot (45) 17336
Chordettes, Cadence (EP) CEP 115
*Leiber/Stoller Big Band, Atlantic SP8047
Teenage Flames, Pickwick SPC 3368, P8 1211
Les Jerolas, RCA Victor CGPS 393
Stan Ruffin, The Other Co., TOC-OGH 109X
Buck Owens, Longines Symphonette SYS 5575
Longines Symphonette, Longines Symphonette SYS 5833
Big Wheelie & the Hubcaps, Scepter SPS 5109
The Cheers (1956) Capitol 3353

CHICKEN
(Leiber, Stoller, Rollins)
CHICKEN AND THE HAWK, THE
(UP, UP AND AWAY)
Joe Turner (1955) Atlantic 1080. Also: Atl Sp 33-376
Joe Turner, Milt Jackson & Roy Eldridge, PAB 2310760

CLIMB, THE
*The Coasters (1962) Atco 6234
The Kingsmen, Wand 681
Duane Eddy, RCA LPM-LSP 2648
Forte Four, Decca 32029

COME A LITTLE BIT CLOSER
*Willy & Ruth (1954) Spark 101
Four Coins, Jubilee J4190
Hank Penny & Sue Thompson, Decca 29314 (78)
The Delltones, Leedon LK-302

CORDELIA
CORN WHISKEY
D.W. WASHBURN
*Willy & Ruth (1954) Spark 105
Jimmy Witherspoon (1952) Federal 12107 (78)
The Monkees (1968) Colgems 66-1023
*The Coasters, Date 2-1607. Also: King 6385
Frank Scott, Ranwood 8035

DANCE!
DANCE WITH ME
(Elmo Glick, Lebish, Treadwell, Nahan)
*The Coasters (1958) Atco 6111
*The Drifters (1959) Atlantic 2040. Also: Atlantic (45) 13010, LP 33-8153
The Blendells, Era (45) 032
B.B. King, ABC D709
The Persuasions, MCA 326
The N.Y. Rubber Rock Band, Henry Street HS10002
The Bananas, Much 9918
Perry Como (1957) RCA Victor 47-6991

DANCIN'
DANCIN' JONES
(Leiber, Stoller, Dino, Sembello)
*Dino & Sembello (1974) A&M 3657

DESTINATION LOVE
Wynonie Harris (1956) Atco 6081
Four Coins, Epic 9192
Elvis Presley (1960) RCA Victor LPM 2231

DIRTY DIRTY FEELING
DO YOUR OWN THING
*Brook Benton (1968) Cotillion 45-44007. Also: (LP) SP9002

DON JUAN
DON'T
*La Vern Baker (1961) Atlantic 2099
Elvis Presley (1958) RCA Victor 47-7150. Also: RCA (45) 447-0621, RCA LSP (33) 2075
*Leiber/Stoller Big Band, Atlantic 8047
Sandy Posey, CBS 4-45828
The Teenage Flames, Pickwick SPC 3501

DOWN HOME GIRL
(Leiber & Butler)
*Alvin Robinson, (1965) Red Bird 10-010
*The Coasters, Date 2-1552
The Rolling Stones, London PS-420
Joe Stampley Epic KE33546
Nazareth, A&M/Canada SP4610, A&M SP4610
Felders Orioles, Mercury 1-36656
Astronauts, RCA Victor LPM-LSP 3454

DOWN IN MEXICO
*The Coasters (1955) Atco 6064. Also: (45) 13004, (LP) 33-111, 33-371, Trip TRP 16-7, TRP 1002
Bobby Short, Atlantic 1262
Terry Melcher, RCA (n/a)

*   Produced by Leiber & Stoller
(F)   Foreign release
(n/a) Information not available

DRAW, THE

DRINKIN' FOOL
DRIP DROP

Ella Mae Morse (45) Capitol 3387
Simon Stokes & The Nighthawks, MGM 5E4677
Sherman & The Teenagers (1961) Columbia 4-42054
Big John Greer (1953) RCA 20-5531 (78)
*The Drifters (1958) Atlantic 1187. Also: (45) 13011, (LP) SP 33-375
Dion Di Mucci, Columbia (45) 13-33220
Dion & The Belmonts, Warner Bros. 2664
*Kenny Chandler (1961) UA 342
*Jay & The Americans, UA UAL 3222

DRUMS

EASYVILLE (Instr.)
(Leiber, Stoller, Bernal)
EVERYBODY'S WOMAN
EVERY MINUTE OF THE DAY

*Gil Bernal (1954) Spark 102

*The Coasters (1968) Date 2-1607
*Frankie Marshall (1956) Atco 6076
The Diamonds, Mercury (45) 71021
Margie Rayburn, Liberty F55043 (45)

FALLING

FAMOUS LAST WORDS
FANCY MEETING YOU HERE
FANNIE LOU
FAREWELL

*Sammy Turner (1960) Big Top (45) 3061. Also: (LP) 12-1301
Julius La Rosa (1957) RCA Victor 47-6998
*The Cheers (1955) Capitol 3146

*Frankie Marshall (1956) Atco 6070
*Willie & Ruth (1954) Spark 101
Connie Russell, Capitol F3137 (45)
Jimmy Witherspoon (1954) Federal 12155 (78)

FAST WOMEN & SLOE GIN
FEELS SO GOOD
(Leiber, Stoller, Dino, Sembello)
FINDERS KEEPERS
FLESH, BLOOD AND BONES
FLIP OUR WIGS
FLYING

*Dino & Sembello (1974) A&M SP3657

*The Crescendos (1956) Atlantic 1109
Little Esther (1952) Federal 12108 (78)

Milt Trenier (1953) RCA Victor 20-5487 (78)
Carmen McRae (1967) Atlantic SP8143
*Leslie Uggams, Atlantic SP8196
Amos Milburn (1952) Aladdin 3125 (78)
Chris Connor, Atlantic 45-2017

FLYING HOME
(Music: Goodman, Hampton. Lyric: Leiber, Stoller)
FOOLS FALL IN LOVE

The Drifters (1957) Atlantic 1123. Also: (45) 13139, Atco LP SP 33-375
Jacky Ward, Mercury (45) 35003, (LP) SRM 1-1170
Elvis Presley, Pickwick (LP) CAS2533, DL2-5001, CBS 7014
Four of A Kind, Melba 117 (45)
*Sammy Turner, Big Top 12-1301
Tony Travis (1957) Verve (45) 10061

FOOTSTEPS
FRAMED

*The Robins (1954) Spark 107. Also: Atco 143
The Coasters, (EP) Atco 4503, (LP) Atco 101
(The Sensational) Alex Harvey Band, Atco 18148
Ritchie Valens, Del-Fi (45) 4106, (LP) 1201
Burton Cummings, Portrait 34698
Jerry Reed, RCA Victor APL1-2516, LSP4596
Cheech & Chong, Ode 66124, (LP) SP 77040
Canned Heat, U.A. LA-049
Bill Haley & The Comets, Quality BM738 (F)
Phil Gulley, Decca 29288 (78)
The Darts, (United Artists) Magnet 850

GEE GOLLY
GET HIM
(Russell, Passman, Elmo Glick)
GET OFF MY WAGON
GIRL WHO LOVED THE MAN WHO ROBBED THE BANK AT SANTA FE (AND GOT AWAY), THE
(Leiber, Stoller, Wheeler)
GIRLS, GIRLS, GIRLS

*The Coasters (1958) Atco 6111
*The Exciters (1963) U.A. 604

*Linda Hopkins (1954) Forecast F-5002
Hank Snow (1963) RCA Victor 47-8151

*The Coasters (1962) Atco 135
Elvis Presley, RCA Victor LSP 2621
Roy Hawkins (1951) Modern 842

GLOOM AND MISERY
(a.k.a. THE SNOW IS FALLIN')
GO MOTHER GO
(Leiber, Stoller, Henderson, Henderson)
GUNFIGHTER
(Leiber, Stoller, Wheeler)
GYPSY
(Leiber, Stoller, Berns, Nugetre)
HARD TIMES

Sam "Highpockets" Henderson (1954) Groove G0021

Tommy Roe (1965) ABC 10-696
Jim Ed Brown, RCA LSP/LPM 3853
*Ben E. King (1963) Atco 6275

Charles Brown (1951) Aladdin 3116 (78)
*T-Bone Walker, Reprise sXS6483

HATCHET MAN, THE
HEAVENLY BLUES (instr.)
HELLO, MISS SIMMS (Instr.)
(Leiber, Stoller, Emmanuel)
HELPLESS
(Leiber, Stoller, Dino, Sembello)
HERE HE COMES
(McCoy, Dixon, Elmo Glick)
HEY MISTER
HEY, SUPERSTAR
(Leiber, Stoller, Dino, Sembello)
HIS KISS
(Stoller, Russell)
HOLLERIN' AND SCREAMIN'
HOLY MOMENT
(Leiber, Stoller, Dino, Sembello)
HONEY, CAN I PUT ON YOUR CLOTHES
(Ray, Leiber, Stoller)
HONGRY
HOT DOG
HOUND DOG

*The Robins (1955) Spark 116
*King Curtis (1959) Atco 6152
*Garland The Great (1955) Spark 121

*Dino & Sembello (1974) A&M SP3657

*Ruth Brown (1961) Atlantic 2088

Frances Faye (1953) Capitol 2604 (78)
*Dino & Sembello (1974) A&M 3657

Betty Harris (1964) Jubilee 5465

Little Esther (1953) Federal 12115 (78)

*Dino & Sembello (1974) A&M 3657

Barbra Streisand, Columbia JC 35375

*The Coasters (1960) Atco 6341
Elvis Presley (1957) RCA Victor LSP 1515
*Willie Mae "Big Mama" Thornton (1953) Peacock 1612 (78)
Elvis Presley (1956) RCA 20/47-6604
Bloodstone, London 33 (S)XPS-634
Chanter Sisters, Polydor 33(S)6075
Jerry Lee Lewis, Everest 33(S)298
Little Richard, Cressendo 33(S)9033. Also: Trip 33(S)8013
Jesse Morrison, Abe 33(S)408
Odetta, Vanguard 33(S)VSD-43/44. Also: 33(S)2109
Elvis Presley, RCA Victor (45)447-0608, RCA Victor 33(S)LSP-1707, RCA Victor 33LPM-4088, RCA Victor 33(S)LSP-4428, RCA Victor 33(S)LSP 4776, RCA Victor 33(S)LSP 6020, RCA Victor 33(S)VPQS 608, RCA Victor 33LPM-6401
Shanana, Kama Sutra 33(S)2073
Spinners, Atco 33(S)2-910
"Big Mama" Thornton, Back Beat 33(S)68. Also: Columbia CG-30776, Vanguard 33(S)79351, ABC 33(S)X-784. Duke 33(S)X-73
Utopia, Kent 33(S)566
Jeanette Williams, Back Beat (45)609
"Big Mama" Thornton, Mercury 72981 (45), SR61225 (LP)
*Leiber/Stoller Big Band, Atlantic 8047
White Cloud, Good Medicine GMLP 3500
Billy Starr, Imperial 8186 (78)
Little Esther, Federal 12126 (78)
Eddie Hazelwood, Intro 6069 (78)
Betsy Gay, Intro 6070 (78)
Tommy Duncan, Intro 6071 (78)
Jack Turner, RCA Victor 20-5276 (78)
Cleve Jackson, Herald 6000 (78)
Freddy Bell, Tenn 101 (78)
Albert King, Stax STS 2015
Sherbet, Infinity (F) INK5145
Homer & Jethro (HOUN' DAWG) RCA Victor 47-6706
Mickey Katz (YOU'RE A DOITY DOG) Capitol F3607
Billy "Crash" Craddock, ABC/Dot 2082
Eddie Brandon, Atco R1147
Terry Tigre, Gusto SD-9934
Werner Muller/London Festival Orch., London SP44217
Bucky Dee James, Springboard Int'l SPX 6015
Odyssey Singers, World WS-505
John Entwistle, MCA 321
Nighthawks, Adelphi 4110
101 Strings, Alshire S-5297
Uriah Heep, Mercury L7503
Golden Age of Rock n' Roll, Ampex OKAM002073
Scotty Moore, CBS P12488
Sam Singers, CES TA-122
Tim Morgan & Michael Cody, Disneyland 3812
Jimi Hendrix & Little Richard, GRT 059-296

Longines Symphonette, Long. Symph. SYS 5854
The Osmonds, MGM M3JB-5012
Rudie Whaling, Paramount PAS-6068
Helmut Gunter Orch., Pickwick SPI-7010
Jim Breedlove, Pickwick DL2-0376
Conway Twitty, Polydor SE4837
Rock 'n Roll Graffiti, RCA ADL2-0376
Nat Stuckey, RCA ACLI-0780
Growl, Warner Bros. 2209

HUMPHREY BOGART — Joan Morris & William Bolcom, (1978), Nonesuch H-71346

I (WHO HAVE NOTHING) (Mogol, Donida Eng. Lyric: Leiber, Stoller) — *Ben E. King (1963) Atco 6267. Also: (45)13069, (LP)165, Roulette (LP)42032
Tony Allen & the Champs, Specialty (LP) 2129
Shirley Bassey, United Artists (LP)LA111-H2. Also: (LP)LA715-H2. United Artists (LP)6463
John Edwards, Cotillion 33(S)9909
Roberta Flack & Donny Hathaway, Atco 33(S)7216
Lionel Hampton, Bur 33(S)754182
Tom Jones, London (45)5N-59005. Also: Epic 33(S)34383
Terry Knight & the Pack, Abkco 33(S)4222, (45)4005
David T. Walker, Ode 33(S)77020
Maxine Weldon, Milestone 33(S)339
Tom Jones, Parrot 45-40051
Liquid Smoke, Avco Embassy AVE 4522
Dee Dee Warwick, Tuesday D-1
Chambers Bros., Avco AV11013 (LP)
Petula Clark, Warner Bros. WS-1608
Righteous Bros., MGM V-65010
Mariam Love, Capitol 58878
Little Milton, Phonodisc CH1203
Linda Jones, Warner Bros. 2105
Mighty Sam, Bell 11044
Patti Drew, Capitol 71498
Country Mile, Liberty 77918
Pigeons, GRT 19687
Beau Dollar, Starday/King KS1099
Street Noise, Stereo Dimension 2010
Pierre LaLonde & Donald Lautrec, Compo 735
Vicky Sunday, Audio Fidelity AFSD 6245
Society of 7, Universal City US73095
Kaplin Kaye, DJM Rec., DJUS 1010
Barbara Blake & The Uniques, 20th Cent. T462
Hodges, Jones, Smith, 20th Cent., TC 2216
Vanilla Fudge, Scepter, CTM 18007
Rouvaun, RCA LSP 4498

I AIN'T GONNA MAMBO — *Betty Jean Morris (1955), Capitol 3296
I AIN'T HERE — Carmen McRae (1975), Blue Note BLNA 462
Joan Morris & William Bolcom, Nonesuch H-71346
I CAN'T HEAR A WORD YOU SAY — *Ruth Brown (1959), Atlantic 2026
I CAN'T SAY NO — *Myrna March (1963) Roulette 4522
I CRY — *Linda Leigh (1951) Verve 10105X45
Fields & Medera Orch., Catalina 2102
I KEEP FORGETTIN' — *Chuck Jackson (1962) Wand 126
*Procol Harum, Chrysalis 1080
*Myrna March, Roulette R-4522
Long John Baldry, Casablanca NBLP7035
The Checkmates, A&M SP 4183
The Hi-Fi's, Cameo Parkway C349
I MUST BE DREAMIN' — *The Robins (1955) Spark 116
The Cheers, Capitol 3146
*The Coasters, (45) Atco 6321, (LP) Atco 33-101
The Hilltoppers, Dot 15373
I ONLY WANT SOME — *Chris Connor (1960) Atlantic 2053
I REMEMBER — *Peggy Lee (1975) A&M 4547
Joan Morris & William Bolcom, Nonesuch H-71346
I SHALL NOT FAIL — *The Honey Bears (1955) Spark 111
I SMELL A RAT — *Willie Mae "Big Mama" Thornton (1954) Peacock 1632. Also: Back Beat 33(S)68, ABC (45) 1495
Howlin' Wolf, Chess 33(S)50002
Young Jessie, Modern 921 (78)
I STILL LOVE YOU — *Ruth Brown (1956) Atlantic 1113
I WANT TO BE FREE — Elvis Presley (1957) RCA Vic EP4114
Con Archer, Boot BOS 7116
Los Teen Tops, CBS CY3-126
Robert Gordon, Private Stock PS7008
I WANT TO DO MORE — *Ruth Brown (1955) Atlantic 1082

IDOL WITH THE GOLDEN HEAD — *The Coasters (1957) Atco 6098. Also: (45)13005, 33(S)371
David Bromberg Band, Fantasy 33(S)79007
Wolfman Jack, Columbia 33(S)PC-33501
The Persuasions, MCA 326
IF IT'S THE LAST THING I DO — *Frankie Marshall (1956) Atco 6061
IF TEARDROPS WERE KISSES — *The Robins (1955) Spark 110
IF YOU DON'T COME BACK — *The Drifters (1963) Atlantic 2191
I'LL BE RIGHT ON DOWN — *T-Bone Walker, Reprise 6483
Elvis Presley, RCA Victor APL 1-0388
Jimmy Witherspoon (1953) Modern 909 (78)
Damita Jo (1961) Mercury 71840
I'LL BE THERE (King, Jones, Elmo Glick) —
I'LL REMEMBER YOU — *Jay and the Americans (1965) UA 805
I'M A HOG FOR YOU, BABY — *The Coasters (1959) Atco 6146. Also: (45) 13007, (LP) SP33-111
The Persuasions, A&M 3656
Siegal/Schwall Blues Band, Wooden Nickel BWL 1-0554
Canned Heat, Atlantic 7289
Youngbloods, Warner Bros. 2566
Dr. Feelgood, CBS 34419
I'M A WOMAN — Peggy Lee (1962) Capitol 4888. Also: (45) 6191, (LP) Stl857, SM386
Christene Kittrell, Vee Jay 444
Sadie Green, Vanguard 33(S)79184
Jim Kweskin Jug Band, Vanguard 33(S)VSD-13/14. Also: 33(S)79163, 33(S)79270
Maria Muldaur, Reprise 33(S)M54-2194
The Coasters (SHE CAN) Date 2-1607
Sammy Davis & Count Basie (SHE'S A WOMAN) Verve (45) VK-10399, (LP)V/V68605
Fontella Bass, Checker LP2997
Shocking Blue, Quality/Colossus 1114
Marilyn Maye, RCA Victor LSP 4299
Debbie Wagon, CES Recording, TE-7 V2 TR 47
Susan Hudson, CBS 8-50093
Dynamite, Great American Music #GA 200
Fancy, WEA Canada BT 89502
Atlanta Connection, Omega OS1142
American Pick Hit Artists, ARA R-1113
Odyssey Prod. Singers, C-T 106
I'M STUCK ON YOU (Silvester, Simmons, McPherson, Leiber, Stoller) — The Poets (1966) Red Bird 10-046 (45)
The Insiders, Red Bird 10-055 (45)
IS THAT ALL THERE IS? — *Leslie Uggams (1968) Atlantic 8196
*Peggy Lee, Capitol 6161, 33(S)SM-386
Tony Bennett, Columbia 33(S)CG-33612
Guy Lombardo, Capitol 33(S)SM-340
Sacha Distel (F) RCA 2C-006-100 721M
Joan Morris & William Bolcom, Nonesuch H-71346
Jim Bailey, UA S-5642
Sidney Miller, Gregar 71-0501
Ron Frangipane, Mainstream MRL-300
Ornella Vanoni (E POI TUTTO QUI?) (F)Aristone ARLP12068
Hildegarde Neff, (F) (n/a)
Maxine Brown, Plantation PLP 521
Julie Andrews/Carol Burnett, CBS S31153
Ferrante & Teicher, UA 8220/K0220
Midnight Voices, GRT 041 35503
Norrie Paramor, Polydor 24-6006
IS THIS GOODBYE? — *Linda Hopkins (1954) Forecast F-5002 (78)
IT — Jimmy Witherspoon (1954) Federal 12180
IT'S A MIRACLE — *The Honey Bears (1954) Spark 104
IT'S BEEN SO LONG — Jo Stafford (1959) Columbia 4-41517
IT'S MY TURN TO CRY (Leiber, Stoller, Garfield) — *Jay & the Americans (1962) UA479
IT'S SO EXCITING — *The Exciters (1963) UA604
I'VE GOT THEM FEELIN' TOO GOOD TODAY BLUES — *Peggy Lee, A&M SP4547
Joan Morris & William Bolcom, Nonesuch H-71346
JACK-O-DIAMONDS — Jacki Fontaine (1954) Forecast 102 (78)
*Ruth Brown, Atlantic 45-2026
JAILHOUSE ROCK — Elvis Presley (1957) RCA 47-7035, EPA 4114, (45)447-0619 (LP) CPLI-0606, (LP) ANLI-0971, (LP) CPLI-1349, (LP) LSP-1707, (LP) APL2-2587, (LP) LPM-4088 (LP) LPM-6401
Jeff Beck, Epic (LP) BXN-26478, (LP) BG-33779
Johnny Cougar, MCA (LP) 2225

Merle Haggard, MCA (LP) 2314
Jerry Lee Lewis, SUN (LP) 124
Shanana, Kama Sutra (LP) 2034, (LP) 2073
Z.Z. Top, London (LP) PS-656
Mind Garrage, RRCA 479812
Albert King, Stax STS 2015
Johnny & Edgar Winter, Blue Sky P234033
*Leiber/Stoller Big Band, Atlantic 8047
Nighthawks, Adelphi 4110
101 Strings, Alshire S-5296
Golden Age of Rock 'n Roll, Ampex 3KAM052073
Gord Tracey/Constellations, Audat/Afton 477-9019
David Cassidy, Bell 1312
Los Teen Tops, CBS CY-3-126
Sam Singers, CES TA-122
Billy "Crash" Craddock, Capitol ST-11758
Jim Breedlove, Keel D82-0376
Bobby Hackey, London SDSC 045113
The Osmonds, MGM M3JB-5012
Tony Osborne & Orch., Mach 8 Tape ME-13
Jony Ussery, Phonogram SRM-1-671
Teenage Flames, Pickwick SPC 3368
Dickie Goodman, Private Stock CR 6000
The Sound Effects, QMO 116
Rock 'n Roll Graffiti, RCA ADL2-0376
Manny Perez, RCA DBLI-5140
Enriquez Guzman, Raff RF 9001
Big Wheelie & the Hubcaps, Scepter SPS 5109
Bucky Dee James, Springboard Int'l SPB 4080
Merle Kilgore, Starday/King SLP479
Sandy Nelson, United Artists UALA 2466
Odyssey Singers, World Studios WS-505

JUICY
(Stoller)
Willie Bobo (1967) Verve VK 10482, LLP V6-8685
Monguito Santamaria, Fania LP338

JUMP THE CANYON
(Leiber, Stoller, Dino, Sembello)
*Dino & Sembello (1974) A&M SP 3657

(SHE'S) JUST ANOTHER GIRL
*Mike Clifford (1962) UA489

JUST LIKE A FOOL
*The Robins (1955) Spark 122. Also: Atco 6059

JUST SAY THE WORD
*Frankie Marshall (1955) Spark 117

JUST TELL HER, JIM SAID HELLO
Elvis Presley (1962) RCA 47-8041, 47-0637, (LP) LSP 3921
*Gerri Granger (JUST TELL HIM JANE SAID HELLO) Big Top 45-3150

KANSAS CITY
Little Willie Littlefield (K.C. LOVING) (1952) Federal 12110 (78), 12351 (45)
Ray Anthony, Ranwood (LP) 8082
Beatles, Capitol (LP) ST-2358, (LP) SKBO-11537
Bill Black Combo, Hi (LP) 32023
David Bromberg, Columbia (LP) KC-32717, (LP) PC-34467
James Brown, Polydor (LP) 6054
Butts Band, Blue Thumb (45)252
Ace Cannon, Hi (LP) 32007
Roy Clark, Dot (LP) 26005
Dion, Laurie (LP) 2019
Barbara Fairchild, Columbia (LP) KC-33058
Wilbert Harrison, Fury 1023. Also: ABC (45) 2524 MCA (LP) 2-8008, Sue SSLP8801, Roulette (LP) 112, Roulette (LP) 42029, Trip TRP (LP) TOP-50-2
Albert King, Utopia (LP) Cy12-2205
Furry Lewis, Fantasy 24703
Little Milton, Checker (LP) 3012
Little Richard, Specialty (LP) 2136
Papa Joe's Music Box, Ranwood (LP) 8128
Cheryl Poole, Paula (LP) 2205
Muddy Waters, Chess (LP) 60035
Jimmy Witherspoon, Prestige, (LP) 7713
Memphis Slim, Crescendo (LP) 10002
Rockin' Ronald, End E-1043 (45)
Beatles (45) Capitol 6066
Little Richard, Specialty 664
James Brown, King 45-6086, (LP) 1020
Hank Ballard, King 45-15025
Beatles, Lingasong LSZ7001
Chris Connor, Atlantic 8061
Steve Lawrence (n/a)
Sammy Davis, Jr., Reprise RS6131
Lee Castle & Jimmy Dorsey Orch., Epic LN3681
Bill Haley & The Comets, Warner Bros. 1831

*Jay & The Americans, United Artists, UAL3222
Lowell Fulson, Festival FR 1031
Peggy Lee, Capitol T1671
Trini Lopez, Reprise R6103
Lou Rawls, Capitol SWBB-261
Libby Titus, Columbia 34152
Joe Williams & Count Basie (n/a)
*T-Bone Walker, Reprise 6483
*Leiber/Stoller Big Band, Atlantic 8147
Fats Domino, ABC Paramount 10596
Herman n' Hermits, MGM SE4282
Al Caiola, United Artists S6586
Mets 1969, Atlantic LP1969
Marvin Montgomery, Capitol BT1982
Dick Dale, Capitol ST1930
Sam Butera, Capitol T1521
Wanda Jackson, Capitol ST1511
Mark Murphy, Capitol T1299
Bobby Paris, Capitol 45-57538
Cliffy Stone, Capitol ST00323
Freddy & Dreamers, Capitol T1630
Johnny Robinson, Columbia BN26528
Georgia Gibbs, Columbia LN24059
Lee Castle, Columbia LN3681
Billy Strange, Point PS326
Everly Bros., W.B. W1578
Frances Faye, Crescendo PS92
Joey Dee, Reprise R25173
Rocky Olson, Chess 1723
Pat Boone, Dot/Famous 25594
Alexys, Dot/Famous 25713
J. F. Murphy & Salt, Electra ET85024
Gene Bricken, Response 165-70071
Shirley Ellis, Congress 3002
Booker Ervin, Liberty 10127
Sandy Nelson, Liberty 9345
Julie London, Liberty 12347
Crickets, Liberty LRP7372
Spike Jones, Liberty 3349
Marvin Jenkens, London GS34001
Jan & Dean, Liberty LRP3314
Tom Jones, London ML001001
Jerry Jaye, London HL12038
Billy Lee Riley, Mercury MG20965
Les Flames, Olympia OLJ109
Roy Drusky, Mercury MG20883
The Applejacks, London 3401
Norman Lee, Marion 1019
Scatman Crothers, Motown M8777
Los Reneldes Del Rock, Orfeon 1064
Jimmy Ricks, Jubilee, 5GS8021
Bob Wills, Kapp KL1506
David Lloyd, Polydor 242-209
Nashville Gold, Evolution Athena 6004
J. Lawrence Cook, Q.R.S. 9691
Wayne Versage, Birchmont BM520
Herb Alpert, Quality 1710X
Marty Wilson, Fox TFM 3101
Chubby Checker, Parkway PSP7036
Clyde McPhatter, Mercury MG20655
Al Hirt, RCA FTP1305
Marilyn Maye, RCA PRS416
Stan Worth, RCA LSP2939
Ann-Margret, RCA LSP2399
The Senate, RCA PCS1301
Nashville All Stars, Royal 63A
Leon McAuliffe, ABC 394
Carl Mann, Sun 9330
Hal Singer, King KSD 1075
Nashville Country Singers, Mt. Dew S7035
Sunset Blues Band, United Artists 5254
Brenda Lee, MCA 32330
Johnny Rivers MCA MCR-R-1088
Nancy Adams, Mega M31 1018
Gordon Jenkins, Romulus RQ 5015
Ron McFarlin, Round Robin 3-S1

KEEP IT UP
KEEP ON ROLLIN'
*The Soul Brothers (1964) Blue Cat 107
*The Coasters (1962) Atco (LP) 135, Atco EP 6192

KING CREOLE
Elvis Presley (1958) RCA LSP 1884

KING SOLOMON'S BLUES (Instr.)
*Gil Bernal (1954) Spark 106

KISSIN' BOOGIE
Preston Love (1952) Spin 102 (78) (Voc. Beverly Wright)

LADY LIKE
*The Coasters (1960) Atco 6341

LADY WANTS TO TWIST, THE
Steve Lawrence (1962) Columbia 4-42396

LAST LAUGH BLUES   Little Esther & Little Willie (1952) Federal 12108 (78)

LAST MILE, THE   Jimmy Witherspoon (1953) Federal 12138 (78)
LET'S BRING BACK
WORLD WAR I   Joan Morris & Bill Bolcom (1978) Nonesuch H-71346
LIPS   Roy Hamilton (1958) Epic 5-9274
    *Azie Mortimor, Big Top 3041
LITTLE EGYPT   *The Coasters (1961) Atco 6192. Also: (45) 13004, (LP) 33-371, Atlantic SD8193, Trip 16-7, Atco (LP) 33-135
    Kaleidescope, Island 9462
    Elvis Presley, RCA LPM 4088, RCA LSP 2999
    Ray Stevens, Barnaby 5010, Monument SLP 18115
    Downliners Sect, Mercury (n/a)
    The Cliche's, Mills MAARCMA 1530

LITTLE WHITE SHIP, A   *Peggy Lee (1975) A&M SP4547
LOLA   *Bob London (1955) Spark 109. Also: Dot 15442
    *The Coasters, Atco LP101
    Jean Houben, Richmond B-20055
    Tohama (F) Decca 9.22.520

LONGINGS FOR A
SIMPLER TIME   *Peggy Lee (1975) A&M SP4547
    Joan Morris & William Bolcolm, Nonesuch H-71346

LOOP-DE-LOOP MAMBO   *The Robins (1954) Spark 107
    *The Coasters, Atco LP 101, EP4503
    Gary Crosby, Decca 29378 (78)
    Jay Jerome and Orch., Teen T102
    Four Escorts, RCA 20/47-5886, 20 5886 (78)
    Billy May, Capitol 2948 (78)

LORELEI   *Lonnie Donegan (1960) Atlantic 2081
LOVE ME   *Willie & Ruth (1954) Spark 105
    Billy Eckstein, MGM 11855 (78)
    Georgia Gibbs, Mercury 70473 (78)
    Five DeMarco Sisters, Decca 29299 (78)
    Elvis Presley, RCA EPA 992, LSP 1382, LSP 1707, CPLI-0606, LSP 4776, VPSX 6889, SPLI 0341
    Eddie Brandon, Artco R1147
    Terry Tigre, Starday/Gusto 50993X
    Fats Domino, Birchmont BM 726, ABC 479
    The Searchers, Sire 147-3705
    Sam (The Man) Taylor, MGM SE3783
    Dick Slocum & The Storm Kings, ABS W230
    Johnny Mann, Liberty LT 7198
    Allman & Woman, Warner Bros. 3120
    Homesteaders, Homstead HT0014
    Connie Russell, Capitol 2933 (78)
    Kay Brown, Crown 127 (78)
    The Four Escorts, RCA Victor 20/47-5886
    Jimmie Rodgers Snow, RCA 20/47-5986 (45), 20/5786 (78)
    Barry Frank, Bell 19
    Dave Burgess, Tops R298
    Vic Corwin, Puccio 354
    Marvin Lockard, Gateway 1198
    Loren Becker, Waldorf 33-176
    *Jackson Bros., Atco 45-6139
    Eddy Arnold, RCA LSP/LPM 2268
    Johnny Burnette, Liberty LRP 3179/LSP 7179
    Bruce Channel, Smash MGS 27008/SRS 77008
    The R.P.M.'s, Port 70032
    Pat Boone, (45) Dot 16525, (LP) Dot DLP3501
    Sal Corrente, Roulette 4673
    Woodside Sisters, "X" 0049 (78)
    Billy Williams Quartet, Coral 61264 (78)
    The American Pick Hit Artists, Assoc. Rec. Artists C-1094
    Ruth Ann Simpson, Spartan of Canada P1407

LOVE POTION #9   *The Clovers (1959) United Artists 180. Also: UAL 3099/UAS 6099, UALA 256, UAM20023, UAS 21023, (45) UA-XW133-A. Atco SP 33-374. MCA (LP) 2-8001
    *The Coasters, King 1146, 6385, Gusto 274
    Los Hooligans, Oregon 1062
    The Searchers, RCA RD518202, Kapp (LP) 1431/3431, Kapp (45) KSB27
    Enoch Light, ABC RSSD 979, Command RS882SP
    Dave Lewis, Jerden 7006
    Sam The Sham & The Pharaohs, MGM E4314
    Don Costa, United Artists UAL 3196-6196
    Casey Jones & The Governors, Mercury 36522
    Boss Guitars, Kapp KL 1427
    Jewel Aikens, Era EL 110
    The Ventures, Liberty BLP 2033
    Gary Lewis, Liberty LRP 3408/7408

The Surfaris, Decca DL4614
The Surfriders, Vault V105
The Curios, Seaburg D116
*Elkie Brooks (LP) A&M 4631
The Searchers (LP) Pye 501, Also: Sir H-3705 (LP)
Johnny "Hammond" Smith, (LP) Prestige 7705
Tijuana Brass, (LP) A&M 4110, (LP) A&M 4245

LOVEY   *The Clovers (1960) United Artists 209. Also: UAL 3099/UAS 6099

LOVING YOU   Elvis Presley (1957) RCA Victor 47-7000
    *Leiber/Stoller Big Band, Atlantic 8047
    Guy & Ralna, Ranwood 8134 (LP)
    Jesse Morrison, Abet 9462 (45), Abet 408 (LP)
    Elvis Presley, RCA ANLI-0971 (LP), LPM-6401, LSP 1515
    Glen Campbell, Capitol SWBC 11707
    American Pickhit Singers, Amer. Pick Hits APH-003
    Nat Stuckey, Pickwick ACL 0533
    Union Station Singers, Union Station SAC-24
    Donna Fargo, Warner Bros. 3099

LOVIN' JIM   Little Mickey Champion (1952) Modern (78) 855
LUCKY LIPS   Ruth Brown (1957) Atlantic 1125, Atco (45) 13146
    Cliff Richard, Epic 5-9597
    Gale Storm, Dot 45-15539

LUMP IN MY THROAT   Little Willie Littlefield (1951) Modern (78) 837
MAINLINER   Little Esther (1952) Federal 12100
MIDNIGHT TOWN,
DAYBREAK CITY   *Roy Hamilton (1963) MGM K13157
(WHEN SHE WANTS
GOOD LOVIN') MY BABY   *The Coasters (1957) Atco 6098
COMES TO ME   Delbert McClinton, DOT (ABC) D959
    Chicago Loop, Dynovoice 226
MY BLIND DATE   *Jaye P. Morgan (1958) RCA Victor 47-7178
MY BOY JOHN   *Baby Jane & The Rockabyes (1962) UA560
    Joey Dee (n/a)
    Steve Lawrence (1961) United Artists 335
MY CLAIRE DE LUNE   *Jay & The Americans, United Artists 626, UAL3222(LP)
    *Anthony Newley, London 3361
    Troy Cory, Cinema Prize 1686
    George Feyer, Cadence 403
    *Steve Rossi, Red Bird 10-023
    *Dino & Sembello (1974) A&M SP3357

NEIGHBORHOOD
(Leiber, Stoller, Dino, Sembello)
NIGHT BIRD   *Elkie Brooks (1977) A&M 4631
(Leiber, Stoller, Gage, York)
NIGHT MARE   Willie Mae "Big Mama" Thornton (1953) Peacock 1612 (78)
NOSEY JOE   (Bull) Moose Jackson (1952) King 4524 (78)
    Chuck Murphy, Coral 60674 (78)
NUMERO UNO (Instr.)
(Stoller)   *Mike Stoller & The Stoller System (1968) Amy 11039
OH, MOTHER, DEAR   Jimmy Witherspoon (1953) Modern 909 (78)
MOTHER
ON BROADWAY   *The Drifters (1963) Atlantic 2182. Also: Atco
(Leiber, Stoller, Mann,   13013 (45), 8153 (LP), Trip TOP-16-6 (LP)
Weil)   Bobby Darin, Capitol
    Illinois Jacquet, Cadence 722 (LP)
    Johnny Keatin, London SP-44072 (LP)
    David T. Walker, Ode 77011 (LP)
    George Benson, Warner Bros. 2WB 3139
    Gary Le Mel, Vee Jay 648
    Barry Mann, New Design 2-30876
    Eric Carmen, Arista AQ-4057 (LP)
    Percy Faith, Columbia 30330
    The Jazz Crusaders, MCA ST20175
    Livingston Taylor, Capricorn SD863
    John Brown Jr.'s Gogo Music, Pye/Phonodisc GH502
    O'Donel Levy, Groove Merchant Int'l GM507
    Jerry Williams, Spindizzy (Columbia) KZ 31404
    Reuben Wilson, United Artists UA BST 84295
    Ray Anthony (n/a)
    Nancy Sinatra, RCA P8S5134
    The Coasters, Starday/King KLP 1146
    Tony Christie, MCA 17021
    Nell Aspero, Fretone FR-014
    David Barretto, Phonogram 73639
    Clyde McPhatter, Candelite 8818
    Jess Roden, Island ILPS 9286
    Buddy Rich Pickwick GM 3307
    Lou Rawls, Capitol SLB8802/83
    Long John Baldry, GM Rec., GMS 9045

ON THE HORIZON | Jim Gold, Tabu BQL1-2308-A
| The Lettermen, Capitol SM-11678 8M
ON THE ROAD AGAIN | *Ben E. King (1961) Atco 6194, 33-13
(Leiber, Stoller, Dino, Sembello) | *Dino & Sembello (1974) A&M 3657

ONE BAD STUD | *The Honey Bears (1954) Spark 104
ONE FINE GAL | Jimmy Witherspoon (1953) Federal 12128 (78)
ONE KISS | *The Robins (1955) Spark 113
ONE KISS LED TO ANOTHER | *The Coasters (1956) Atco 6073, (LP) Atco 101
| Delbert McClinton, ABC (Dot) 959
| Sunny Gale, Decca 9-30063
ONLY IN AMERICA | *Jay & The Americans (1963) United Artists 626
(Leiber, Stoller, Mann, Weil)
AN OPEN FIRE | Johnny Mathis (1959) Columbia CL1270, EPB12531
OVER AND OVER | *Frankie Marshall (1956) Atco 6076
PAPA DADDY | *Ruth Brown (1959) Atlantic 2035
PAST, PRESENT AND FUTURE | The Shangri-Las (1966) Red Bird 10-068
(Leiber, Butler, Morton)
PEARL'S A SINGER | *Dino & Sembello (1974) A&M SP3657
(Leiber, Stoller, Dino, Sembello)
| *Elkie Brooks, A&M 4631 (45), A&M 1935 (LP)
PERFECT WAVE, THE | *Mike Stoller & The Stoller System (1968) Amy 11039
(Instr.) (Stoller)
POISON IVY | *The Coasters (1959) Atco 6146. Also: (45) 13005, (LP) 371, MCA 2-8007 (LP), Roulette 112 (LP), Roulette 42029 (LP)
| Redbone, Epic PEG-33456 (LP)
| Rolling Stones, London 2PS-626-27 (LP)
| Odyssey, Hollbrooke HB6002
| *Leiber/Stoller Big Band, Atlantic 8047
| Enriquez Guzman, Raff RF 9001
| Los Rebeldes del Rock, Orfeon 106 4 OLMS 4
| Let The Good Times Roll, Ampex 3BELO59002
| The Kingsman, Scepter CTN18002
PROFESSOR HAUPTMAN'S PERFORMING DOGS | *Mike Stoller & The Stoller System (1968) Amy 11027
(Instr.) (Stoller)
PROFESSOR HAUPTMANN'S PERFORMING DOGS | *Peggy Lee (1975) A&M 4547
| Joan Morris & Bill Bolcom, Nonesuch H-71346
QUE PASA, MUCHACHA | The Cheers with Les Baxter (1956) Capitol 3409
RAT RACE | *The Drifters (1963) Atlantic 2191
(Leiber, Stoller, McCoy)
READY TO BEGIN AGAIN (MANYA'S SONG) | *Peggy Lee (1975) A&M 4547
| Bette Midler, Atlantic 2-9000
| Joan Morris & William Bolcom, Nonesuch H-71346
REAL UGLY WOMAN | Jimmy Witherspoon (1951) Modern 20-821 (78)
RECKLESS | *Bob London (1955) Spark 109
| Suzi Miller, London 45-1648
RIOT IN CELL BLOCK #9 | *The Robins (1954) Spark 103
| Commander Cody & The Lost Planet Airmen, Paramount (LP)1017, Warner Bros. (LP)2LS-2939
| Johnny Winter, Columbia PC/PCQ-32715 (LP)
| Vicki Young, Capitol 2865 (78)
| Little John & The Rumblers, Downey 119
| The Crew, Strand 25001
| Wanda Jackson, Capitol 4503
| Major Rowley, Bell (Amy) 934
| The Beach Boys (STUDENT DEMONSTRATION TIME), Reprise 6433
| Darts, United Artists 850
| Dr. Feelgood, Columbia PL34098
| Pagliaro, Columbia FS 90320
RUBY BABY | The Drifters (1956) Atlantic 1089. Also: Atco 33-375, Atlantic (45) 13014
| Billy "Crash" Craddock, ABC (45) 2755, ABC (DOT) (LP)2082
| Dion, Columbia (45) 13-33063, (LP)PG-33390
| Ronnie Hawkins, Roulette (LP) 42045, (45) R-4249
| Wednesday, Private Stock QA510
| The Odyssey, Group TEJ-700
| Jack Johnson, World Sound Factory 4050
| Dion & The Belmonts, Warner Bros. 2664
| Frut, Westbound 2008
| Sammy Mason, Sundance Volume 19

RUN RED RUN | The Beatles, Polydor/Canada 2371 051
| Frut, Chess WB 2008
| *The Coasters (1959) Atco 6153, LP 33-135
| Phil Harris, Reprise R-20, 117
SANTA CLAUS IS BACK IN TOWN | Elvis Presley (1957) RCA EPA 4108, LOC 1035, LPM1951
| Mae West, Dagonet DG-4
SATURDAY NIGHT DADDY | Little Esther & Bobby Nunn (1952) Federal 12100 (78)
SAVED | *La Vern Baker (1961) Atlantic 2099, (LP)8078, Atco (45) 13002, Atco SP 33-372
| The Band, Capitol (LP) SW-11214
| *Elkie Brooks, A&M 4631 (LP)
| Brenda Lee, MCA 2233 (LP)
| Elvis Presley, Vic LPM-4088
| Eddie Haddad, MGM 14749
| Mama Lion, Famous FPS2713
| Young Rascals, DLP 253
| Judy Henske, Reprise S6203
| Lulu, Atco SP33-330
| Southern Fried, Cream 1018
| The Blood Brothers, Warner Bros. J15115
SAY IT | *Peggy Lee (1975) A&M SP 4547
SEARCHIN' | *The Coasters (1957) Atco 6087, 33-371, Atlantic (45)13003, Original Sound (LP) 8858
| The Crewcuts, Warwick (n/a)
| Bloodstone, London XPS-634 (LP)
| Ace Cannon, Hi 32072/73 (LP), Hi 21274 (45
| Gloria Gaynor, MGM M3G-4982 (LP)
| Hampton Hawes, Contemporary 7631 (LP)
| McCoy Tyner, Impulse 79 (LP)
| Music, Eleuthera ELS 3601
| Buzzy Linhart, Kama Sutra 2042
| Jim Croce, Lifesong LS 45001 (45), LS900 (LP)
| Spencer Davis, United Artists LA433
| Johnny Rivers, United Artists 225, LA075
| Kitty Wells, Epic P13613
| Otis Blackwell, Inner City IC 1032
| Mugwumps, Warner Bros. 7018
| Jack Eubanks, Monument 45-451-J
| *Alvin Robinson, Tiger TI-104
| Wanda Jackson, Pickwick JS6123
| Greaseball Boogie Band, GRT of Canada 9230-1042
| Melba Montgomery, Elektra 4527
SHACK DADDY | *Betty Jean Morris (1955) Capitol 3296
SHADOW KNOWS, THE | *The Coasters (1958) Atco 6126, (LP) 533-111
| Marrion Brown, Reprise RE 9139
| Commander Cody & His Lost Planet Airmen, Warner Bros. 2883
SHAKE 'EM UP AND LET 'EM ROLL | Earl Richard (1968) United Artists 50462
| Kenny Ball (F) Pye 7N17944
| George Kent, Shannon SH840
| Bruce Nelson, Royal American RA74A
SHE'S NOT YOU | Elvis Presley (1962) RCA Victor 47-8041, (45) 447-6637 (LP) LSP 2765, LPM 6401
(Leiber, Stoller, Pomus)
SILVER SEA HORSE | *Mike Stoller & The Stoller System (1968, AMY 11027
(Instr.)
SMOKEY JOE'S CAFE | *The Robins (1955) Spark 122, Atco 6059, Atl (45)13106
| *Leiber/Stoller Big Band, Atlantic 8047
| McCoys, Bang 213 (LP)
| Louden Wainwright, III, Columbia C-31462 (LP)
| Ray Charles (1953) Swingtime 326 (78)
SNOW IS FALLING (a.k.a. GLOOM AND MISERY)
SOME CATS KNOW | *Leslie Uggams (1968) Atlantic 81968
| *Peggy Lee, A&M 4547, (45) 1771
SOME OTHER GUY | *Richie Barrett (1962) Atlantic 2142
(Leiber, Stoller, Barrett) | The Searchers (n/a)
| Freddie & The Dreamers, Capitol XAX 2676
| Les Lionceaux, London 125501
| Stardust, Arista 5000
| Big Three, London DPA 030090
SONG FROM MY HEART | *Frankie Marshall (1956) Atco 6061
SORRY BUT I'M GONNA HAVE TO PASS | *The Coasters (1958) Atco 6126
| Elton Anderson, Lanor 514
SOUL PAD | *The Coasters (1968) Date 2-1552
SPANISH HARLEM | *Ben E. King (1960) Atco 6185
(Leiber, Spector) | Henry Jerome, Liberty UXS 71
| Long John Baldry, Janus JX25 7002
| Los Indios Tabajaras, RCA LSP 4615
| Lucky Peterson, Today TLP 1002
| Pepe Leon, Polydor 2414079
| The Crusaders, Motown M796
| Billy May, RCA RDCS 22

Leon Russell, Shelter SR2108
Enrique Guzman, Columbia CLT 7097
Lawrence Lucie, Toy T1001
Morton Downey, Private Stock PS45168
Sam Buttera & The Witnesses, Dot DLP3381
Kai Winding, Verve VG 8639
Ronnie Aldrich, London SP-44070
Ray Anthony, Ranwood 8082 (LP)
Chet Atkins/Boston Pops, Victor LSC-3104 (LP)
Vikki Carr, Columbia C-31040 (LP)
Frank Chacksfield, London SP-44141
King Curtis, Atco 33-266
Exotic Guitars, Ranwood 8104 (LP)
Aretha Franklin, Atlantic (45)13062, (LP)QD-8305, Atlantic 18204 (LP)
Bobbi Humphrey, Blue Note BN-LA699-G (LP)
*Ben E. King. Atlantic (45)13068, Atco 33-165, 33-133, Atlantic 18198 (LP), Specialty 2SP-9104
Love Child's Afro-Cuban Blues Band, Midsong International BKLI-2292 (LP)
Mamas & The Papas, Dunhill 50006 (LP), 50038 (LP)
Buddy Merrill, Accent 5040 (LP)
Tony Mottola, Project 3 QD-5062 (LP)
Laura Nyro/LaBelle, Columbia PC-30987 (LP)
Boots Randolph, Monument MP-8604 (LP)
Sonny Stitt, Cadence 60040 (LP)
Tennessee Guitar, SSS International 10 (LP)
Andy Williams, Columbia CG031064 (LP)
*Jay & The Americans, United Artists UAL 3222
Lloyd Price, ABC 336
Santo & Johnny, Amcan CA 137
Jimmy Justice, Kapp KL130S/KS3308
Gene McDaniels, Liberty LRP 3275
Dalida, Verve V/V6 8467
Clyde McPhatter (n/a)
The Challengers, Atlantic LP 103
Andre Kostelanetz, Columbia CL 2138/CS 8938
Bobby·Vee, Liberty LRP 3385
Sounds, Inc., Liberty L 55729
Danny Davis & Orch., Kapp KL1393/KS3393
The Invictas, 20th Century Fox, TFM 3132/TFS 4132
Percy Faith, Columbia CL2279/CS9079
Bobby Gordon & Orch., Decca 31713
Tom Jones, Parrot, PA61004/PAS 71004
Tommy Leonetti, RCA LPM/LSP 3404
John Barry, United Artists UAL3424
John Keating, London SP44072
Don Randi, London SBG 38
Al Caiola, United Artists UAL 3473/6473
Trini Lopez, Reprise RS 6215
Anita Kerr Orch., Warner Bros. WS1640
Freddie Scott, Shout/Bang SLP 501
Roosevelt Grier, MGM K13840
Living Marimbas, RCA (n/a)
Provocative Strings of Zacharias, RCA LPM/LSP 3597
Arthur Alexander, Monument 1060
The Clean Sweeps, Phillips 40556
The Tennessee Three, CBS 4-44264
Herb Alpert & The Tijuana Brass, A&M 8502
Sonny Charles & The Checkmates, Ltd., A&M 1127
Adam Ross Percussion, Kapp K 12049
N.Y. Electric String Ensemble, Columbia CS9992
Anthony Ventury und sein orch., RCA KXL1 0212
Roberto Delgado, Polydor 249 330
Love Strings, Ampex MCS 1009
James Last, Polydor 2414 029
Jumbo Sterlings All Stars, Phonodisc MALS 1286
Pretty Purdie, Mega M51-5001
Carmen Cavallaro, Ampex E1001
Brazil Country, Crown City CCR 111
Longines Symphonette, Longines Symphonette SYS 5814
The Undivided, London, SCL-002073
Geoff Love & His Orch., Quality RS106
101 Strings, Arc SF 8002
Dave Lewis, Jerden 7006
The Mariachi Brass, London WP1842
Vi Velasco, MTA 103
Dave Lewis, Quality V. SV1791

SQUEEZE ME

STAND BY ME
(King, Elmo Glick)

STAY A WHILE

STEADFAST, LOYAL
AND TRUE
STEWBALL
STRAWBERRY STOMP
(Instr.)
STREET LIGHTS
STRIKING ON YOU,

George Renan & His Manhattan Stars, Jay Gee JGM/SLP700
Garry Blake & His Music, Capitol YAX 1320
Eddie Heywood, London LRP3279
Cliff Richard w/The Shadows & Norris Paramor & His Orch., Capitol, YAX 2344
Adam Ross Percussion, Kapp K-12049
The Fiesta Brass, Columbia P2-12932
Manuel & His String Play, Ampex 13-4299
Les Reed & His Orch., London Des 18007
Freddie Scott, Ampex SHX 501
The Keating Sound, London SP44072
Hubert Smith Trio, Edmar 1025
Orch. Del Oro, Miller St. Son 100
Jean-Michel Defaye & Orch., Mercury 24790
Jonah Jones, Capitol 38636
Luis Mariano, Capitol 7XLA 2861
Werner Muller, London TP 2521
Sam Butera & The Witnesses, Dot DLP 3381/25381
Lloyd Price, Spartan Abc366
Roger Johnson, Roll Around
John Barry, United Artists, AM13002
Arena Brass, Columbia LN-24039
Jimmy Justice, Kapp KL 1308
Tony Orlando/Dawn, Elektra 45344
Tennessee Guitars, Power Pak PO-253
Phil Spector, Warner Bros. OP-2508
Milt Trenier (1953) RCA Victor 20/5275 (78)
*Ben E. King (1961) Atco 6194, Also: 33-165, 33-142, Atlantic (45) 13069
Otis Redding (n/a)
Johnny Adams, Chelsea 525 (LP)
Allan Clarke, Asylum 7E-1056 (LP)
Ry Cooder, Reprise 2254 (LP)
Fantastic Johnny C., Phil. L.A. of Soul 4000 (LP)
Narvel Felts, ABC/Dot 2070 (LP)
Earl Grants, MCA 246 (LP), Decca 25674 (45), MCA 2-4059 (LP)
John Lennon, Capitol 6244 (45), Cap SK-3419 (LP)
Little Milton, Checker 2995 (LP)
Carl McKnight, Ranwood 8159 (LP)
Junior Parker, Duke X-83 (LP)
Johnny "Hammond" Smith, Prestige 7494 (LP)
Sonny & Cher, Atco 2-804 (LP)
Ike & Tina Turner, United Artists UA-La064-G2
Cassius Clay, Columbia 4-43007
Don Shirley, Cadence 1420 (45)
David & Jimmy Ruffin, Soul S-35076 (45)
Wilbert Harrison, Sue 5SLP8801
*Jay & The Americans, United Artists UAL 3222
Spyder Turner, MGM K13617
Gene Chandler, Vee Jay VJLP/VJSR 1040, Scepter PS 704
Southern Fried, Mercury SR61338
Billy Mize, United Artists 6781 (LP)
David & Jimmy Ruffin, Motown 55728
Pretty Purdie, Mega M51-5001
Barbara Lewis, Atlantic SD8286
Earl Van Dyke, Motown 715
Shirley Scott & The Soul Saxes, Ampex B4/81532
Gary Ruffin, CES Records TR50
Andriano Celectano (F) Peters International PILPS 4030
Ray Garnet, Assoc. Rec. Artists 00578
Serge Fontane, Trans World Rec. Amusement 16004
Johnny Colon & Orch., Cotique CQ1014
Jimmy Ruffin, Motown 728
Odyssey C-T 107
Mike Martin, Dellwood GNS 36080
Longines Symphonette, Long. Symph. SYS 5817
Dimension Sound, TEJ J-1000
*The Clovers (1959) United Artists 180 (45). Also: UAL 3099/UAS 6099 (LP), UA-XW133-A ($')
Elvis Presley (1958) RCA Victor LSP 1884

*The Coasters (1960) Atco 6168, 33-135
*Gil Bernal (1954) Spark 106

Little Esther (1953) Federal 12122 (78)
Little Willie Littlefield (1952) Federal 12101 (78)

BABY
SWEET DREAMS   *T-Bone Walker, Reprise 6483
TAKE IT LIKE A MAN   *The Crescendos (1956) Atlantic 1109, 2014
    Gene Pitney (1962) Musicor 1020
    Walker Bros., London/Canada MGS 27082, SRS 67082
TAKE MY LOVE   Mabel Scott (1953) Brunswick 84001 (78)
TANGO   *Peggy Lee (1975) A&M SP4547
    Diana Markovitz, Kama Sutra KSBS2614
    Joan Morris & William Bolcom, Nonesuch H-71346
TEACH ME HOW TO SHIMMY   *Isley Bros. (1961) Atlantic 2092
    The Coasters (n/a)
TEARS OF JOY   *Linda Hopkins (1953) Crystalette 2001 (78)
    Etta James (n/a)
    Bertice Reading, RCA Victor 20-5567 (78)
TELL ME MORE   *Jaye P. Morgan (1958) RCA Victor 47-7178
TEN DAYS IN JAIL   The Robins (1953) RCA Victor 20 5489 (78)
THAT IS ROCK & ROLL   *The Coasters (1959) Atco 45-6141
    *The Coasters, Atco 33-111
    Sylvester & The Hot Band, Blue Thumb 3097342
    Porky Chedwick, Atlantic LP8100
    Chesterfields, A&M SP 6500
THAT'S WHAT THE GOOD BOOK SAYS   Bobby Nunn & "The Robbins" (1951) Modern 807 (78)
THERE GOES MY BABY (Nelson, Patterson, Treadwell, Leiber, Stoller)   *The Drifters (1959) Atlantic 2025. Also: (45) ATL13011 (LP) ATL 8153, 42029, Atco 33-375, Atco 2-504
    Jay & The Americans, United Artists 50858
THREE COOL CATS   *The Coasters (1959) Atco 6132
THREE CORN PATCHES   *T-Bone Walker (1973) Reprise 2X56483
    Elvis Presley, RCA Victor APL1-0388
THE TIME LOSER   *Linda Hopkins (1953) Chrystalette 2001 (78)
THUMBIN' A RIDE   *The Coasters (1961) Atco 6186
    Jackie Lomax, Apple 23 (F)
TONIGHT I'M SINGING JUST FOR YOU (Leiber-Wheeler)   *Billy Edd Wheeler (1965) Kapp 655
TOO BAD SWEET MAMA HENDERSON (Henderson, Leiber, Stoller)   Sam "Highpockets" Henderson (Shorty Rogers) (1954) Voc: Billy Black (Jerry Leiber), Groove G-0021 (78)
TOO MUCH JELLY ROLL   *Little Brother Brown (1951) Okeh 6835 (78), Voc: Irlton French
    Floyd Dixon, Alladin 3111 (78)
A TOUCH OF HEAVEN   *Mister Ruffin (1955) Spark 115
    Dick Lee, RCA X4Y-10145
TREAT ME NICE   Elvis Presley (1957) RCA Victor 47-7035, (45)44-7-0619 (LP) RCA LSP 1707, LPM 6401
    Tommy James, Fantasy 9509
    Golden Ring, ARC AS832
    Conway Twitty, Candelite CMI 3266
    Werner Muller/London Fest. Orch., London SP44217
TREE STUMP JUMP (Leiber, Stoller, Emanuel)   *Garland The Great (1955) Spark 121
TRICKY DICKY   *Richie Barrett (1962) Atlantic 2142
    The Searchers (n/a)
TRIP WITH ME   Nancy Wilson (1970) Capitol ST 429, (LP) 2831
TROUBLE   Elvis Presley (1958) RCA Victor LSP 1884
    Suzi Quatro, Bell 1313
    Johnny Hallyday, Philips B373.091F (F)
    The Darts, United Artists 850
    Johnny Farago, Les Disque Nobel NBL 508/9
    Osmonds, MGM M8LT 4826
    Scrubbaloe Caine, RCA APLI-0263
TURN THE LAMPS DOWN LOW   Little Esther & Little Willie (1953) Federal 12115 (78)
TURTLE DOVIN'   *The Coasters (1955) Atco 6064, (LP) 33-371
WAILIN' DADDY   Mabel Scott (1953) Brunswick 84001 (78)
WELL I'M DANCIN'   *Ocie (O.C.) Smith (1960) Big Top 3039
WHADAYA WANT   *The Robins (1955) Spark 110
    *The Cheers, Capitol 3019
    The Charms, Deluxe 6080 (78), King 4318
    Jack Cardwell, King 1454
WHAT ABOUT ME   Larry Evans (1956) Fabor 4009
WHAT ABOUT US   *The Coasters (1959) Atco 6153, 33-135
WHAT IS THE SECRET OF YOUR SUCCESS   *The Coasters (1957) Atco 6104
WHAT TO DO WITH LAURIE (Leiber, Stoller, Wheeler)   *Mike Clifford (1962) United Artists 557
WHAT'S WRONG WITH ME & YOU (Gluck, Goldstein, Elmo Glick)   *Babs Tino (1961) Kapp 388
WHERE'S THE GIRL   *Jerry Butler (1964) Vee Jay 534, (LP) 1076

    *Ben E. King, Atco 45-6596
    *Jay & The Americans, United Artists UAL3562, UAS6562
    Buddy Greco, Reprise 0551, Warner Bros. J-4609, (LP) 6256, (LP) 6230
    *Steve Rossi, Red Bird 10-029
    Freddy Scott, Colpix CP 461
    Dorsey Burnette, Reprise 2107, (45) 208

THE WHIP (Instrumental) (Leiber, Stoller, Bernal)   *Gil Bernal (1954) Spark 102
WHIPPER SNAPPER   LaVern Baker (1958) Atlantic 1189
WHISTLE FOR HAPPINESS   Peggy Lee (1969) Capitol (45) SM386, (LP) ST1857
WHOA!   *The Honey Bears (1955) Spark 111
WHY OH WHY (Leiber, Stoller, Marshall)   *Frankie Marshall (1956) Atco 6070
WILL YOU LOVE ME STILL   June Valli (1957) RCA Victor 47-6852
    Dion & The Belmonts, Laurie (LP) 2016
WRAP IT UP   *The Robins (1954) Spark 103
WRITE TO ME (Elmo Glick, Isley)   *The Isley Bros. (1961) Atlantic 2110
YAKETY YAK   *The Coasters (1958) Atco 6116, Also: (45) 13006, (LP), 111, (LP) 371, (LP) 2-504
    Boots Randolph, Monument (45) 1909, (LP), MC-6600, (LP) MG-7602
    Shanana, Kama Sutra (LP) 2034, (LP) 2073, (LP) 2-2609, (45) 81 (Radio Active Gold)
    Bloodstone, London (LP) PS-665, P5665
    Sandy Nelson, United Artists (LP) UA-LA491-G, UALA 491, UALP 1240
    Eric Weisburg & Deliverance, 6P6354, 8-50072
    Ray Stevens, Barnaby BR5010, Also: Monument SLP18115
    Las Jerolas, RCA CGPS 393
    Sam The Sham, MGM K13863
    Brian Poole & Tremeloes, Decca (EP) DFE 8566 (F)
    West Road Blues Band, Island ILPS 9418
    Frankie Avalon, Phonogram DJR 9504
    El Coco, Quality AVI 1039
    The Teenage Flames, Pickwick SPC 3601
    Joe Turner, Polydor BTS 9009
    Super Black Band #2, Atlantic BT 29009
    Joe Liggens (1954) Mercury 70440
YEAH, YEAH, YEAH / YES   *Ben E. King (1962) Atco 6215, Also: 33-132
    *Jay & The Americans, Liberty UAL 3222, SUS 5278, UA 504 (45)
YOU CAN'T LOVE 'EM ALL (Lieber, Stoller, Russell, Nugetre)   Solomon Burke (1964) Atlantic 8096
    The Drifters (n/a)
YOU DID SOMETHING FOR ME   *Elkie Brooks (1977) A&M SP 4631, Also: (45) 1935
YOU LAUGH   Jack Jones (1958) Capitol 3991
YOU STILL LOVE HIM (McCoy, Elmo Glick)   *Roy Hamilton (1962) MGM K13138
YOU TOOK MY LOVE TOO FAST (Stoller, Darnell)   Little Esther & Bobby Nunn (1953) Federal 12122 (78)
YOU'LL BE THERE (Leiber, Stoller, Relf)   Clyde McPhatter (1957) Atlantic 1158
YOU'LL NEVER LEAVE HIM (Stoller, Russell)   The Isley Bros. (1963) United Artists 659
    Lulu (n/a)
YOUNG AND IN LOVE   Tony Castle (1958) East West 107
YOUNG BLOOD (Leiber, Stoller, Pomus)   *The Coasters (1957) Atco 6087, (45) 13003, (LP) 111, (LP) 371, Also: Trip (LP) Top-16-7
    Bad Company, Swan Song (45) 70108, (LP) 8415
    Flash Cadillac, Epic (LP) KEG-33465
    Concert For Bangla Desh (Leon Russell) Apple STCX 3385
    The Darts (United Artists) Magnet UALA 850-G
    The Righteous Bros., Capitol/EMI of Canada Haven 7014
    *The Isley Bros. (1961) Atlantic 2110
YOUR OLD LADY (Isley, Curtis, Elmo Glick)
YOU'RE KILLING ME   Milt Trenier (1953) RCA Victor 20-5487 (78)
YOU'RE THE BOSS   *LaVern Baker & Jimmy Ricks (1961) Atlantic 2090

A Chronological Listing of Records Produced by Leiber and Stoller

1953

Linda Hopkins	*Three Time Loser	Crystalette 2001
	*Tears of Joy	
Willie Mae "Big Mama" Thornton	*Hound Dog	Peacock 1612
	*Night Mare	

1954

The Cheers	*Bazoom (I Need Your Lovin')	Capitol 2921
	Arrivederci	
The Cheers	*Can't We Be More Than Friends	Capitol 3075
Linda Hopkins	*Is This Goodbye	Forecast F-5002
	*Get Off My Wagon	
Willie Mae "Big Mama" Thornton	*I Smell A Rat	Peacock 1632
Willy & Ruth	*Come a Little Bit Closer	Spark 101
	*Farewell	
Gil Bernal	*Easyville	Spark 102
	*The Whip	
The Robins	*Riot in Cell Block #9	Spark 103
	*Wrap It Up	
The Honey Bears	*One Bad Stud	Spark 104
	*It's a Miracle	
Willy & Ruth	*Love Me	Spark 105
	*Cordelia	
Gil Bernal	*King Solomon's Blues	Spark 106
	*Strawberry Stomp	
The Robins	*Loop-de-Loop Mambo	Spark 107
	*Framed	

1955

Ruth Brown	*I Want to Do More	Atlantic 1082
	Old Man River	
The Cheers	*Fancy Meeting You Here	Capitol 3146
Betty Jean Morris	*Shack Daddy	Capitol 3296
	*I Ain't Gonna Mambo	
Bob London	*Reckless	Spark 109
	*Lola	
The Robins	*If Teardrops Were Kisses	Spark 110
	*Whadaya Want?	
The Honey Bears	*Whoa!	Spark 111
	*I Shall Not Fail	
The Sly Fox	*Alley Music	Spark 112
The Robins	*One Kiss	Spark 113
	I Love Paris	
Mister Ruffin	*A Touch of Heaven	Spark 115
	Bring It on Back	
The Robins	*The Hatchet Man	Spark 116
	*I Just Be Dreamin'	
Frankie Marshall	*Just Say the Word	Spark 117
	No One Else Will Ever Know	
Ernie Andrews	Soft Winds	Spark 118
	In the Still of the Night	
Garland the Great	*Tree Stump Jump	Spark 121
	*Hello, Miss Simms	
The Robins	*Smokey Joe's Cafe	Spark 122
	*Just Like a Fool	

1956

Frankie Marshall	*If It's the Last Thing I Do	Atco 6061
	Song from My Heart	
The Coasters	*Turtle Dovin'	Atco 6064
	*Down in Mexico	
Frankie Marshall	*Fannie Lou	Atco 6070
	*Why Oh Why	
The Coasters	*One Kiss Led to Another	Atco 6073
	Brazil	
Frankie Marshall	*Every Minute of the Day	Atco 6076
	*Over and Over	
The Crescendos	*Finders Keepers	Atlantic 1109
	*Sweet Dreams	
Ruth Brown	*I Still Love You	Atlantic 1113

1957

The Coasters	*Searchin'	Atco 6087
	*Young Blood	
The Coasters	*(When She Wants Good Lovin') My Baby Comes to Me	Atco 6098
	*Idol with the Golden Head	
Young Jessie	Shuffle in the Gravel	Atco 6101
	Make Believe	
The Coasters	*What Is the Secret of Your Success	Atco 6104
	Sweet Georgia Brown	
The Coasters	*The Coasters	Atco LP 33-101

1958

	*Lola	
The Coasters	*Dance	Atco 6111
	*Gee Golly	
The Coasters	*Yakety Yak	Atco 6116
	Zing! Went the Strings of My Heart	
The Coasters	*The Shadow Knows	Atco 6126
	*Sorry But I'm Gonna Have to Pass	
The Drifters	*Drip Drop	Atlantic 1187
	Moonlight Bay	
Young Jessie	That's Enough for Me	Atlantic 2003
	Margie	
The Notables	Moonlight and Roses	Big Top 3001
	Under the Bridges of Paris	
The Knott Sisters	Sunglasses	Big Top 3003
	Undivided Attention	
Bobby Pedrick, Jr.	White Bucks and Saddle Shoes	Big Top 3004
	Stranded	
Sammy Turner	Sweet Annie Laurie	Big Top 3007
	Thunderbolt	
Varetta Dillard	The Rules of Love	RCA Victor 47-7144
	Star of Fortune	
Jaye P. Morgan	*My Blind Date	RCA Victor 47-7178
	*Tell Me More	
David Hill & His Men	*Cha! Bull! (The Crowd)	RCA Victor 47-7322
	A Promise of Things to Come	

1959

The Coasters	*Charlie Brown	Atco 6132
	*Three Cool Cats	
Jackson Brothers	Tell Him No	Atco 6139
	*Love Me	
The Coasters	*Along Came Jones	Atco 6141
	*That Is Rock and Roll	
The Coasters	*I'm a Hog for You, Baby	Atco 6146
	*Poison Ivy	
King Curtis	*Heavenly Blues	Atco 6152
	Restless Guitar	
The Coasters	*What About Us	Atco 6153
	*Run Red Run	
The Drifters	*There Goes My Baby	Atlantic 2025
	Oh, My Love	
Ruth Brown	*I Can't Hear a Word You Say	Atlantic 2026
	*Jack O'Diamonds	
Ruth Brown	*Papa Daddy	Atlantic 2035
	I Don't Know	
The Drifters	*Dance with Me	Atlantic 2040
	(If You Cry) True Love, True Love	
Mickey & Kitty	My Reverie	Atlantic 2046
	Buttercup	
The Drifters	This Magic Moment	Atlantic 2050
	Baltimore	
Sammy Turner	Lavender Blue	Big Top 3016
	Wrapped Up in a Dream	
Ellen Van Valen	I Really Don't Want to Know	Big Top 3026
	I Wish I Didn't Love You So	
Sammy Turner	Always	Big Top 3029
	Symphony	
Sammy Turner	I'd Be a Fool Again	Big Top 3032
	Paradise	
Sammy Turner	I Want to Be Loved	Big Top 3038
	Goodnight, Irene	
Sammy Turner	Lavender Blue Moods	Big Top LP 12-1201
	Honey	
	I Can Dream, Can't I	
The Clovers	*Love Potion #9	United Artists 180
	*Stay A While	

1960

The Coasters	Besame Mucho (Part I)	Atco 6163
	Besame Mucho (Part II)	
Rocky Matero	Lawdy Miss Clawdy	Atco 6165
	All Alone	
The Coasters	*Stewball	Atco 6168
	Wake Me, Shake Me	
The Coasters	Shopping for Clothes	Atco 6178
	The Snake & The Bookworm	
Ben E. King	*Spanish Harlem	Atco 6185

*Songs written by Jerry Leiber and/or Mike Stoller, jointly, individually, and/or in conjunction with other writers.

Artist	Title	Label/Number
The Coasters	First Taste of Love	Atco LP 33-123
	One by One	
	But Beautiful	
	Satin Doll	
	Gee Baby, Ain't I Good to You	
	Autumn Leaves	
	You'd Be So Nice to Come Home to	
	Moonlight in Vermont	
	Moonglow	
	Easy Living	
	The Way You Look Tonight	
	Don't Get Around Much Anymore	
	Willow Weep for Me	
	On the Sunny Side of the Street	
Chris Connor	*I Only Want Some	Atlantic 2053
	That's My Desire	
Joe Turner	Chains of Love	Atlantic 2054
	My Little Honey Dripper	
The Drifters	Lonely Winds	Atlantic 2062
	Hey, Senorita	
The Drifters	Save the Last Dance for Me	Atlantic 2071
	Nobody but Me	
Lonnie Donegan	*Lorelei	Atlantic 2081
	Junco Partner	
O.C. Smith	*Well, I'm Dancing	Big Top 3039
	You Are My Sunshine	
Azie Mortimer	*Lips	Big Top 3041
	Wrapped Up in a Dream	
Sammy Turner	*Fools Fall in Love	Big Top 3049
	Stay My Love	
Sammy Turner	*Falling	Big Top 3061
	The Things I Love	
The Clovers	*Lovey	United Artists 209

1961

Artist	Title	Label/Number
The Coasters	*Thumbin' a Ride	Atco 6186
	Wait a Minute	
The Coasters	*Little Egypt	Atco 6192
	*Keep on Rolling	
Jimmy Ricks	Young at Heart	Atco 6193
	Hi-Lilli, Hi-Lo	
Ben E. King	*Stand By Me	Atco 6194
	*On the Horizon	
The Coasters	*Girls, Girls, Girls (Part I)	Atco 6204
	*Girls, Girls, Girls (Part II)	
Ben E. King	Here Comes the Night	Atco 6207
	Young Boy Blues	
The Coasters	*Bad Blood	Atco 6210
	(Ain't That) Just Like Me	
Ben E. King	*Spanish Harlem*	Atco LP 33-133
	Amor	
	Sway	
	Come Closer to Me	
	Perfidia	
	Granada	
	Sweet and Gentle	
	Quizas, Quizas, Quizas	
	Frenesi	
	Souvenir of Mexico	
	Besame Mucho	
	Love Me, Love Me	
The Drifters	I Count the Tears	Atlantic 2087
	Suddenly There's a Valley	
Ruth Brown	*Here He Comes	Atlantic 2088
	Sho' Nuff	
La Vern Baker & Jimmy Ricks	*You're the Boss	Atlantic 2090
	I'll Never Be Free	
Isley Brothers	*Teach Me How to Shimmy	Atlantic 2092
	Jeepers Creepers	
The Drifters	Some Kind of Wonderful	Atlantic 2096
La Vern Baker	*Saved	Atlantic 2099
	*Don Juan	
Isley Brothers	Standing on the Dance Floor	Atlantic 2100
	Shine On, Harvest Moon	
The Drifters	Please Stay (Don't Go)	Atlantic 2105
Isley Brothers	*Write to Me	Atlantic 2110
	*Your Old Lady	
The Drifters	Sweets for My Sweet	Atlantic 2117
	Loneliness or Happiness	

Artist	Title	Label/Number
The Drifters	Room Full of Tears	Atlantic 2127
	Somebody New Dancin' With You	
Leiber-Stoller Big Band	*Yakety Yak*	Atlantic LP SD-8147
	*Yakety Yak	
	*Loving You	
	*Black Denim Trousers and Motorcycle Boots	
	*Bazoom	
	*Poison Ivy	
	*Kansas City	
	*Jailhouse Rock	
	*Smokey Joe's Cafe	
	*Don't	
	*Charlie Brown	
	*Hound Dog	
Babs Tino	*What's Wrong with Me and You	Kapp 388
	If Only for Tonight	
Anthony Newly	*My Clair de Lune	London 3361
	What Kind of Fool Am I	
Johnny Ray	How Many Nights, How Many Days	United Artists 341
	I'll Bring Along My Banjo	
Kenny Chandler	*Drums	United Artists 342
	The Magic Ring	
Jay & The Americans	Tonight	United Artists 353
	The Other Girls	
Annie Williams	I've Got a Man	United Artists 374
	Playboy	

1962

Artist	Title	Label/Number
Ben E. King	*Yes	Atco 6215
	Ecstasy	
The Coasters	*The Climb	Atco 6234
	*The Climb (Instr.)	
The Coasters	*Bull Tick Waltz	Atco 6251
	The P.T.A.	
The Coasters	*Coast Along with the Coasters*	Atco LP 33-135
	My Babe	
The Drifters	When My Little Girl Is Smiling	Atlantic 2134
	Mexican Divorce	
Richie Barrett	*Some Other Guy	Atlantic 2142
	*Tricky Dicky	
The Drifters	Sometimes I Wonder	Atlantic 2151
	Jackpot	
Jack Jones	Pick Up the Pieces	Kapp 461
	Gift of Love	
The Shirrelles	It's Love That Really Counts	Scepter 1237
Tommy Hunt	I Just Don't Know What to Do with Myself	Scepter 1236
	And I Never Knew	
Tony Middleton	Drifting	United Artists 410
	Memories Are Made of This	
Jay & The Americans	She Cried	United Artists 415
	Dawning	
Jeff Barry	Welcome Home	United Artists 440
	(We Got Love) Money Can't Buy	
Leiber-Stoller Orch.	*Cafe Espresso	United Artists 441
	Blue Baion	
The Shepard Sisters	Lolita Ya Ya	United Artists 456
	Marvin	
Johnny Maestro	Before I Loved Her	United Artists 474
	Fifty Million Heartbeats	
Jay & The Americans	*It's My Turn to Cry	United Artists 479
	This Is It	
Paul Dino	That's How I Miss You	United Artists 481
	Tonight's the Night	
Mike Clifford	*(She's) Just Another Girl	United Artists 489
	Close to Cathy	
Jay & The Americans	*Yes	United Artists 504
	Tomorrow	
Billy Edd Wheeler	Not Me	United Artists 517
	Truckstop Romance	
The Exciters	Tell Him	United Artists 544
	Hard Way to Go	
Marv Johnson	Everyone Who's Been in Love With You	United Artists 556
	Keep Tellin' Yourself	
Mike Clifford	*What to Do with Laurie	United Artists 557
	That's What They Said	
Ferrante & Teicher	Theme from *Lawrence of Arabia*	United Artists 563

Jay & The Americans	She Cried	United Artists LP UAL3222
	*Drums	
	*Kansas City	
	Save the Last Dance for Me	
	*Stand By Me	
	Moon River	
Irene Reid	*My Heart Said (The Bossa Nova)	Verve VK10286
	Meditation	
Chuck Jackson	*I Keep Forgettin'	Wand 126
	Who's Gonna Pick Up the Pieces	

1963

Ben E. King	*I (Who Have Nothing)	Atco 6267
Ben E. King	*Gypsy	Atco 6275
	I Could Have Danced All Night	
The Drifters	Up on the Roof	Atlantic 2162
	Another Night with the Boys	
The Drifters	*On Broadway	Atlantic 2182
	Let the Music Play	
The Drifters	*If You Don't Come Back	Atlantic 2191
	*Rat Race	
Gerri Grainger	*Just Tell Him Jane Said Hello	Big Top 3150
Garnell Cooper & The Kinfolks	Green Monkey	Jubilee 45-5445
	Long Distance	
Ray Peterson	Give Us Your Blessing	Dunes 2025
	Without Love (There Is Nothing)	
Billy Edd Wheeler	*After Taxes	Kapp 550
	Blistered	
Billy Edd Wheeler	A New Bag of Songs	Kapp LP KS3351
	Jack and the Doc's Daughter	
	The Bachelor	
	Hot Dog Heart	
	Blue Roses	
	Jackson	
	Desert Pete	
	The Reverend Mr. Black	
	Anne	
	Coal Tattoo	
	Winter Sky	
Roy Hamilton	*You Still Love Him	MGM 13138
	Let Go	
Roy Hamilton	*Midnight Town, Daybreak City	MGM 13157
Myrna March	*I Can't Say No	Roulette 4522
	*I Keep Forgettin'	
Tippie & The Clovers	*Bossa Nova, Baby	Tiger 201
	*The Bossa Nova (My Heart Said)	
Jay & The Americans	What's the Use	United Artists 566
	Strangers Tomorrow	
The Exciters	He's Got the Power	United Artists 572
	Drama of Love	
The Exciters	Tell Him	United Artists LP UAL 326
	It's Love That Really Counts	
	Say It with Love	
Mike Clifford	One Boy Too Late	United Artists 588
	Danny's Dream	
The Exciters	*Get Him	United Artists 604
	*It's So Exciting	
Jay & The Americans	*Only in America	United Artists 626
	*My Claire de Lune	
Jay & The Americans	Look in My Eyes, Maria	United Artists 669
	Come Dance with Me	
Jay & The Americans	To Wait for Love	United Artists 693
	Friday	
The Exciters	We Were Lovers (When the Party Began)	United Artists 721

1964

The Drifters	I'll Take You Home	Atlantic 2201
	I Feel Good All Over	
The Drifters	In the Land of Make Believe	Atlantic 2216
The Ad Libs	The Boy from New York City	Blue Cat 102
	Kicked Around	
The Soul Brothers	*Keep It Up	Blue Cat 107
	I Got a Dream	
Alvin Robinson	How Can I Get Over You	Blue Cat 108
	I'm Gonna Put Some Hurt	

Joan Toliver	Joan Toliver	Kapp LP K4502
	Ere Job	
	Fisherman's Wife	
	Black Crow Flying	
	Chink-a-Pink	
	Easy Rider Blues	
	The Wayfarer	
	Golden Apples	
	Can Ye Sew Cushions	
	Bones	
	The Flowers Are Blooming Forevermore	
	Ole Hannah, Don't You Rise	
The Dixie Cups	Chapel of Love	Red Bird 10-001
	Ain't That Nice	
Jersey Red	Shine on, Harvest Moon	Red Bird 10-002
	No other Baby	
The Dixie Cups	People Say	Red Bird 10-006
	Girls Can Tell	
The Honeyman	*Brother Bill (The Last Clean Shirt)	Red Bird 10-007
	James Junior	
Alvin Robinson	Fever	Red Bird 10-010
	*Down Home Girl	
The Dixie Cups	You Should Have Seen the Way He Looked at Me	Red Bird 10-012
Election Year 1964	Part I	Red Bird 10-013
	Part II	
The Dixie Cups	Another Boy Like Mine	Red Bird 10-017
	Little Bell	
The Dixie Cups	The Dixie Cups	Red Bird LP 20-100
	Thank You Mama, Thank You Papa	
	All Grown Up	
Bessie Banks	Go Now	Tiger 102
	Sounds Like My Baby	
Alvin Robinson	Something You Got	Tiger 104
	*Searchin'	
Jerry Butler	Need to Belong	Vee Jay LP1076
	Message to Martha	
	How Beautifully You Lie	
	*Where's the Girl	

1965

The Coasters	*Hongry	Atco 6341
	*Lady Like	
Ronnie Mitchell	Having a Party	Blue Cat 111
	I'm Loving You More Every Day	
Alvin Robinson	Bottom of My Soul	Blue Cat 113
	*Down Home Girl	
Steve Rossi	I'll Set My Love to Music	Red Bird 10-023
	*My Claire de Lune	
The Dixie Cups	Iko Iko	Red Bird 10-024
	Gee, Baby, Gee	
Steve Rossi	*Where's the Girl	Red Bird 10-029
The Dixie Cups	I'm Gonna Get You Yet	Red Bird 10-032
	Gee, the Moon Is Shining Bright	
The Poets	Merry Christmas, Baby	Red Bird 10-046
	*I'm Stuck on You	
John Hammond	I Wish You Would	Red Bird 10-047
	I Can Tell	
Sidney Barnes	I Hurt on the other Side	Red Bird 10-054
	Switchy Walk	
The Shangri-Las	*Bull Dog	Red Bird LP 20-101
Steve Rossi	Try to Remember	Red Bird LP 20-106
	How Insensitive	
	My Heart Reminds Me	
	More	
Jay & The Americans	*I'll Remember You	United Artists 805

1968

Mike Stoller and the Stoller System	*Silver Sea Horse	Amy 11027
	*Professor Hauptman's Performing Dogs	
Mike Stoller and the Stoller System	*The Perfect Wave	Amy 11039
	*Numero Uno	
Leslie Uggams	What's An Uggams?	Atlantic LP 33-8196
	What the World Needs Now	
	Any Old Time of the Day	
	In the Land of Make-Believe	
	Let the Music Play	

Artist	Title	Label
	River Deep, Mountain High	
	*Is That All There Is?	
	*Flying	
	*Some Cats Know	
Brook Benton	*Do Your Own Thing	Cotillion 44007
	I Just Don't Know What to Do with Myself	
The Coasters	*Soul Pad	Date 2-1552
	*Down Home Girl	
The Coasters	*D.W. Washburn	Date 2-1607
	*Everybody's Woman	

1969

Artist	Title	Label
Peggy Lee	*Is That All There Is?	Capitol 2602
	Me and My Shadow	

1971

Artist	Title	Label
The Coasters	*D.W. Washburn	King 6385
	*Love Potion #9	

1972

Artist	Title	Label
The Coasters	Cool Jerk	King 6389
	*Talkin' 'bout a Woman	

1973

Artist	Title	Label
Stealers Wheel	Stealers Wheel	A&M LP SP4377
	Stuck in the Middle with You	
	Late Again	
	Another Meaning	
	I Get By	
	Outside Looking in	
	Johnny's Song	
	Next to Me	
	Jose	
	Gets So Lonely	
	You Put Something Better Inside Me	
Stealers Wheel	Everything Will Turn Out Fine	A&M 1450
Stealers Wheel	Ferguslie Park	A&M LP SP4419
	Star	
	Good Business Man	
	Wheelin'	
	Waltz (You Know it Makes Sense)	
	What More Could You Want	
	Over My Head	
	Blind Faith	
	Nothing's Gonna Make Me Change My Mind	
	Steamboat Row	
	Who Cares	
	Back on My Feet Again	
	Everything Will Turn Out Fine	
Eddie James	*Been Down So Long	King 6413
The Coasters	On Broadway	King LP K-1146-498
	*On Broadway	
	Mohair Sam	
	The In-Crowd	
	Down At Poppa Joe's	
	Mustang Sally	
T-Bone Walker (with Dizzy Gillespie, Herbie Mann, Al Cohn, David "Fathead" Newman, Zoot Simms, and The Sweet Inspirations)	Very Rare	
	*Hard Times	
	*Striking on You, Baby	
	*Kansas City	
	*Brother Bill (The Last Clean Shirt)	
	*Been Down So Long	
	*Three Corn Patches	
	Please Send Me Someone to Love	
	Evening	
	The Come Back	
	Your Picture Done Faded	
	Don't Give Me the Runaround	
	Every Day I Have the Blues	
	Person to Person	
	Fever	
	I'm Still in Love with You	
	Just a Little Bit	
	James Junior	
	*If You Don't Come Back	
	Well, I Done Got Over It	
	Stormy Monday	

1974

Artist	Title	Label
Dino & Sembello	Dino & Sembello	A&M LP SP3657
	*Dancin' Jones	
	*Feels So Good	
	*Pearl's a Singer	
	*Jump the Canyon	
	*The Best Thing	
	*A Holy Moment	
	*Helpless	
	*On the Road Again	
	*Neighborhood	
	*Hey Superstar	

1975

Artist	Title	Label
Peggy Lee	Mirrors	A&M LP SP4547
	*Professor Hauptmann's Performing Dogs	
	*I've Got Them Feelin' Too Good Today Blues	
	*Say It	
	*Tango	
	*A Little White Ship	
	*Longings for a Simpler Time	
	*The Case of M.J. (Mary Jane)	
	*I Remember	
	*Ready to Begin Again (Manya's Song)	
	*Some Cats Know	
Procol Harum	Procol's Ninth	Chrysalis LP 1080
	Pandora's Box	
	Fool's Gold	
	Taking the Time	
	The Unquiet Zone	
	The Final Thrust	
	*I Keep Forgetting	
	Without a Doubt	
	The Piper's Tune	
	Typewriter Torment	
	Eight Days a Week	

1976

Artist	Title	Label
Elkie Brooks	Elkie Brooks	A&M LP SP4631
	*Pearl's a Singer	
	*Saved	
	Honey, Can I Put on Your Clothes	
	*You Did Something for Me	
	*Night Bird	
	Spirit Land	
	Sunshine after the Rain	
	*Love Potion #9	
	Mojo Hannah	
	Do Right Woman, Do Right Man	

Photo Credits